Steck-Vaughn

WORLD GEOGRAPHY AND YOU

Vivian Bernstein

Consultant

Jacquelyn Harrison, Ed. D.
Curriculum & Instruction Administrator for Social Studies
Round Rock Independent School District
Round Rock, Texas

STECK-VAUGHN
ELEMENTARY · SECONDARY · ADULT · LIBRARY

A Harcourt Company

www.steck-vaughn.com

ABOUT THE AUTHOR

Vivian Bernstein is the author of *America's Story, World History and You, America's History: Land of Liberty, American Government*, and *Decisions for Health*. She received her Master of Arts degree from New York University. Bernstein is active with professional organizations in social studies, education, and reading. She gives presentations about content area reading to school faculties and professional groups. Bernstein was a teacher in the New York City Public School System for a number of years.

STAFF CREDITS

Executive Editor: Ellen Northcutt
Senior Editor: Martin S. Saiewitz
Design Manager: Rusty Kaim

Photo Editor: Margie Foster
Electronic Production: Jill Klinger

ACKNOWLEDGEMENTS

Cartography: GeoSystems, Inc.
Illustrations: Academy Artworks
Flags: © The Flag Folio
Photography Credits: (KEY: C=Corbis; CB=Corbis-Bettmann; SS=Superstock)
P. 2 © SS; p. 3 Wyoming Division of Tourism; p. 4 (top) © SS, (bottom) © Didier Doryal/Masterfile; p. 7 (left) © J. A. Kraulis/Masterfile, (right) © SS; p. 9 © Charles Krebs/The Stock Market; p. 10 (top) © Hans Blohm/Masterfile, (bottom) CB; p. 11 (both) © Peter Christopher/Masterfile; p. 12 © Jed Jacobson/AllSport; p. 16 © SS; p. 17 © Ron Sanford/The Stock Market; p. 18 (top) © Lloyd Sutton/Masterfile, (left) © SS; p. 19 (right) © Tom Tracy/The Stock Market, (bottom) U.S. Capitol Office of Photography; p. 20 NASA; p. 25 © SS; p. 26 (left) © Thomas Braise/The Stock Market, (bottom) © Sherman Hines/Masterfile; p. 27 (top) © SS, (right) © Patrice Halley/Gamma Liaison; p. 28 (top) © J. A. Kraulis/Masterfile, (bottom) © Andrew Vaughn/; p. 29 © Roland Weber/Masterfile; p. 34 (both) AP/Wide World; p. 35 (top) © SS, (bottom) © Mark Tomalty/Masterfile; p. 36 (top) © SS, (bottom) © Lou Jr. Jacobs/Gamma Liaison; p. 39 (left) © Bo Vince Street/The Stock Market, (right) © W. Bayer/Bruce Coleman, Inc.; p. 42 (top) © Alpamayo John Phelan/DDB Stock Photo, (bottom) © Keith Gunner/Bruce Coleman, Inc.; p. 43 (right) © J. P. Courau/DDB Stock Photo, (bottom) © F. Erize/Bruce Coleman, Inc.; p. 44 (top) © Paulo Fridman/International Stock, (bottom) © M. Joly/DDB Stock Photo; p. 48 The Granger Collection; p. 49 (top) © Bryon Augustin/DDB Stock Photo, (bottom) © D. Donne Bryant/DDB Stock Photo; p. 50 (top) © D. Donne Bryant/DDB Stock Photo, (bottom) © Jerry Cooke/Photo Researchers; p. 51 (top) © D. Donne Bryant/DDB Stock Photo, (right) © Jean-Marc Giboux/Gamma Liaison; p. 52 © Russell/Bruce Coleman, Inc.; p. 57 © Jaris Burger/Bruce Coleman, Inc.; p. 58 (top) © Claude Urraca/Sygma, (bottom) © Silvio/Gamma Liaison; p. 59 (top) © J. C. Carton/Bruce Coleman, Inc., (right) © Inga Spence/DDB Stock Photo; p. 60 © Chuck Mason/International Stock; p. 65 © Gary Williams/Gamma Liaison; p. 66 (left) © Joan Laconetti/Bruce Coleman, Inc., (bottom) © Sullivan & Rogers/Bruce Coleman, Inc.; p. 67 (top) © Jase Azel/The Stock Market, (right) © SS; p. 68 © Buu-Hires/Gamma Liaison; p. 73 © Jonathan Kirn/Gamma Liaison; p. 74 (top) © Paulo Fridman/International Stock, (bottom) © Erwin & Peggy/Bruce Coleman, Inc.; p. 75 (top) © Editora Abril/Gamma Liaison, (bottom) © Gamma Liaison; p. 76 (top) © John Chiasson/Gamma Liaison, (bottom) © Editora Abril/Gamma Liaison; p. 81 © Bruce Coleman, Inc.; p. 82 © Alejandro Balaguer/Sygma; p. 83 (top) © Alejandro Balaguer/Sygma, (bottom) © Jacques M Chenet/Gamma Liaison; p. 84 (top) © J. C. Carton/Bruce Coleman, Inc., (bottom) © Robin Schwartz/International Stock; p. 89 (top) © David Madizon/Bruce Coleman, Inc., (bottom) © Bill Wrenn/International Stock Photo; p. 90 (top) © Francisco Erize/Bruce Coleman, Inc., (bottom) © George Ancona/International Stock; p. 91 (top) © Norman Owen Tomalin/Bruce Coleman, Inc., (bottom) © Buddy Mays/International Stock; p. 92 (top) © Bleibtreu/Sygma, (bottom) © Roberto Arakaki/International Stock; p. 95 (top) © Miwako Ikeda/International Stock, (bottom) © Hilary Wilkes/International Stock; p. 97 © Gian Luigi Scarifiotti/International Stock; p. 98 © SS; p. 99 (top) © J. Messerschmidt/Bruce Coleman, Inc., (bottom) © Phototheque SGM/International Stock; p. 100 (top) © SS, (bottom) © Joachim Messerschmidt/Bruce Coleman, Inc.; p. 104 © Hilary Wilkes/International Stock; p. 105 (top) © Bruce Coleman, Inc., (right) © Richard Folwell/Photo Researchers; p. 106 (both) © C; p. 107 (top) © Gamma Liaison, (right) © SS; p. 113 © SS; p. 114 (left) © John Elk III/Bruce Coleman, Inc., (bottom) © SS; p. 115 (both) © SS; p. 116 (top) © SS, (bottom) © R. T. Nowitz/Photo Researchers; p. 122 (top) © Bouvet/Hires/Merillon/Piel/Gamma Liaison, (left) © C; p. 123 (right) © Anthony Suau/Gamma Liaison, (bottom) © SS; p. 124 (both) © C; p. 125 (top) © David R. Frazier/Photo Researchers, (bottom) © C; p. 130 © Chazot/Explorer/Photo Researchers; p. 131 © H. P. Merten/The Stock Market; p. 132 (top) © C, (left) © Alvero De Leiva/Gamma Liaison; p. 133 (both) © C; p. 138 © CB; p. 139 (right) © Reuters/Pawel Kapczynski/Archive Photos, (bottom) © Simon Fraser/Science Photo Library/Photo Researchers; p. 140 © Sygma; p. 143 (left) © Loubat/Explorer/Photo Researchers, (right) © Vanier/Explorer/Photo Researchers; p. 145 The Granger Collection; p. 146 © Georges Merillon/Gamma Liaison; p. 147 (top) © Brent Winebrenner/International Stock, (bottom) © C; p. 148 (top) © Bill Bachmann/Photo Researchers, (left) © C; p. 152 © J.P. Laffont/Sygma; 153 (top) © Brossard/Explorer/Photo Researchers, (bottom) © Michael Philip Mannheim/International Stock; p. 154 (top) © Kok/Gamma Liaison, (left) © Laski Diffusion/Gamma Liaison; p. 155 (top) © Boutin/Explorer/Photo Researchers, (bottom) © Archive Photos; p. 160 © Wolfgang Kaehler/Gamma Liaison; p. 161 (top) © C, (right) © Ellen Rooney/International Stock; p. 162 (top) © Photo Researchers, (bottom) © James D. Wilson/Gamma Liaison; p. 163 (top) © Osvald/Gamma Liaison, (right) © Francis Apesteguy/Gamma Liaison; p. 164 (top) © CB, (left) © Heidi Bradner/Gamma Liaison; p. 165 © L. Veisman/Bruce Coleman, Inc.; p. 171 (top) © Buddy Mays/International Stock, (right) © Bruce Brander/Photo Researchers; p. 172 © Novosti/Photo Researchers; p. 173 (top) © Jeff Greenberg/Photo Researchers, (bottom) Gamma Liason; p. 178 © Andrew Reid/Gamma Liaison; p. 179 © Art Zamur/Gamma Liaison; p. 180 (top) © Peterson/Gamma Liaison, (bottom) C; p. 185 (top) C, (right) © Chad Ehlers/International Stock; p. 186 (top) © CB, (left) © V. Leloup/Gamma Liaison; p. 187 (top) © Gilles Saussier/Gamma Liaison, (bottom) © Reuters/David Brauchli/Archive Photos.

CONTENTS

Introduction   Getting Started in Geography 1

Unit 1   The United States and Canada 7

Chapter 1   Two Nations of North America 8
Think and Apply: Compare and Contrast 14

Chapter 2   The United States: Land of Variety 15
Biography: Shannon Lucid 20
Think and Apply: Categories 22

Chapter 3   Canada: A Giant Land of Few People 24
Special Places: Montreal 29
Think and Apply: Sequencing 31

Chapter 4   The United States and Canada Work Together 33
Think and Apply: Find the Main Idea 38

Unit 2   Latin America 39

Chapter 5   Land and People of Latin America 40
Think and Apply: Drawing Conclusions 46

Chapter 6   Mexico: A Nation of Contrasts 47
Special Places: Mexico City 52
Think and Apply: Cause and Effect 54

**Chapter 7   Central America: Seven Countries
in the Tropics** 56
Think and Apply: Fact or Opinion 62

Chapter 8   The Caribbean: Hundreds of Beautiful Islands 64
Think and Apply: Sequencing 70

Chapter 9   Brazil: Home of the Amazon Rain Forest 72
Biography: Chico Mendes 76
Think and Apply: Finding Relevant Information 78

Chapter 10   The Countries of the Andes 80
Think and Apply: Categories 86

Chapter 11   Understanding Latin America 88
Think and Apply: Find the Main Idea 94

Unit 3   Western Europe 95

**Chapter 12   Western Europe: The Western Nations
of a Small Continent** 96
Think and Apply: Drawing Conclusions 102

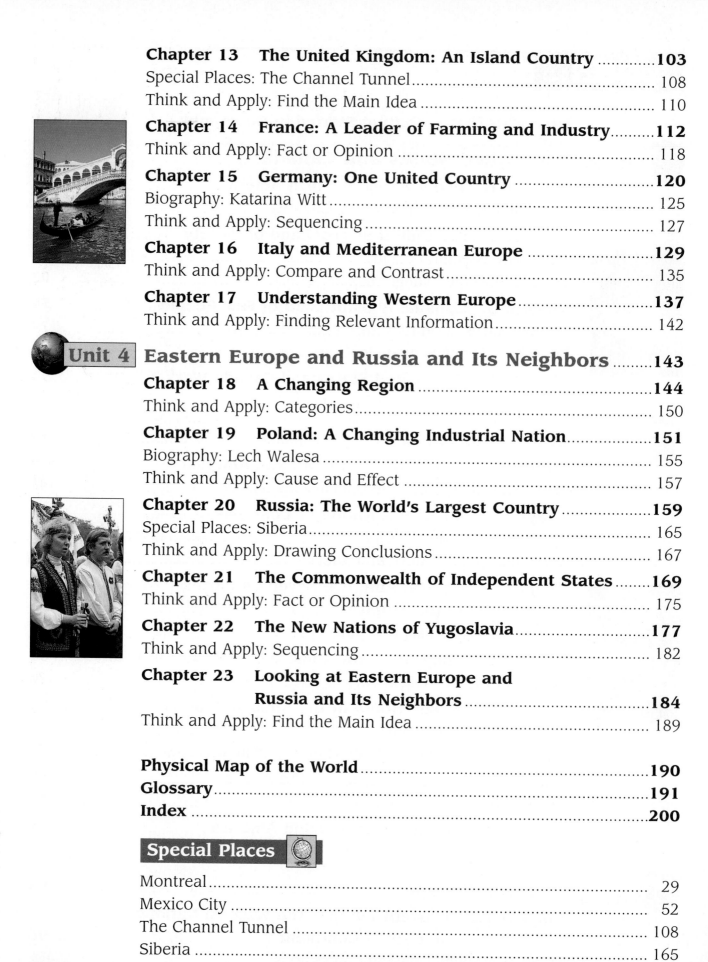

Chapter 13   The United Kingdom: An Island Country **103**
Special Places: The Channel Tunnel.. 108
Think and Apply: Find the Main Idea 110

Chapter 14   France: A Leader of Farming and Industry........**112**
Think and Apply: Fact or Opinion 118

Chapter 15   Germany: One United Country **120**
Biography: Katarina Witt.. 125
Think and Apply: Sequencing 127

Chapter 16   Italy and Mediterranean Europe **129**
Think and Apply: Compare and Contrast... 135

Chapter 17   Understanding Western Europe............................**137**
Think and Apply: Finding Relevant Information 142

Unit 4   Eastern Europe and Russia and Its Neighbors **143**

Chapter 18   A Changing Region **144**
Think and Apply: Categories... 150

Chapter 19   Poland: A Changing Industrial Nation..................**151**
Biography: Lech Walesa 155
Think and Apply: Cause and Effect 157

Chapter 20   Russia: The World's Largest Country **159**
Special Places: Siberia... 165
Think and Apply: Drawing Conclusions... 167

Chapter 21   The Commonwealth of Independent States........**169**
Think and Apply: Fact or Opinion 175

Chapter 22   The New Nations of Yugoslavia.............................**177**
Think and Apply: Sequencing 182

**Chapter 23   Looking at Eastern Europe and
                Russia and Its Neighbors** **184**
Think and Apply: Find the Main Idea 189

Physical Map of the World..**190**
Glossary..**191**
Index **200**

Special Places

Montreal.. 29
Mexico City 52
The Channel Tunnel 108
Siberia 165

Biography

Shannon Lucid.. 20
Chico Mendes 76
Katarina Witt.. 125
Lech Walesa 155

Skill Builder

Using Map Directions and a Compass Rose 23
Reading a Map Key.. 32
Using a Distance Scale.. 55
Locating Places on a Grid 63
Understanding Lines of Latitude.. 71
Understanding Lines of Longitude.. 79
Using Latitude and Longitude.. 87
Reading a Bar Graph 111
Understanding Circle Graphs 119
Reading a Political Map.. 128
Reading a Physical Map 136
Understanding Line Graphs 158
Reading a Statistics Table 168
Understanding a Resource Map.. 176
Comparing Historical Maps.. 183

Maps

Brasília 2
The World: Oceans and Continents...................................... 5
Canada and the United States 9
The United States of America 16
Four Regions of the United States 17
The United States: Using Map Directions and a Compass Rose......... 23
Canada 25
Canada: Reading a Map Key 32
Latin America 41
Northern Hemisphere and Southern Hemisphere................... 41
Mexico.. 48
Mexico: Using a Distance Scale.. 55
Central America 57
The Panama Canal 60
Panama City: Locating Places on a Grid 63
The Caribbean Islands.. 65

Haiti and the Dominican Republic 68
Middle America and the Caribbean: Understanding Lines
    of Latitude 71
Brazil 73
Brazil: Understanding Lines of Longitude 79
Countries of the Andes 82
Andean Countries: Using Latitude and Longitude 87
Western Europe 97
Ocean Currents 98
The United Kingdom 104
Channel Tunnel 108
France 113
Germany 121
Divided Germany and Divided Berlin 121
Germany: Reading a Political Map 128
Portugal, Spain, Italy, and Greece 130
Italy 131
Italy: Reading a Physical Map 136
NATO and the Partnership for Peace 138
The European Union 140
Eastern Europe and Russia and Its Neighbors 145
The Former Soviet Union 146
Poland 152
Russia 160
The Commonwealth of Independent States 170
Ukraine 172
Ukraine: Understanding a Resource Map 176
New Nations of Yugoslavia 178
Yugoslavia in 1945: Comparing Historical Maps 183
Yugoslavia in 1992: Comparing Historical Maps 183
Physical Map of the World 190

Charts, Graphs, and Diagrams

Landforms 3
Four Climate Regions in the Andes 81
Population of the Four Parts of the United Kingdom 111
The Work Force in France 119
Poland's Imports and Exports 158
The Population and Number of Cars for Six Countries 168
Ethnic Groups in Bosnia 179

Getting Started in Geography

Think About As You Read

1. What can you learn by studying world geography?
2. What are the five themes of geography?
3. What are Earth's oceans and continents?

New Words

- geography
- culture
- religion
- themes
- location
- place
- human/environment interaction
- movement
- region
- latitude
- longitude
- landforms
- plateaus
- continents

People and Places

- Brasília
- Brazil
- Atlantic Ocean
- Anápolis
- Pacific Ocean
- Indian Ocean
- Arctic Ocean
- Asia
- Africa
- North America
- South America
- Antarctica
- Europe
- Australia

Where are the longest rivers? How do people live in a desert? Why do people move from one place to another? These are just a few of the questions you will answer as you study world geography.

What Is the Study of Geography?

Geography is the study of the planet Earth. As you study world geography, you will learn what the land looks like in different parts of the world. You will learn how people live in different places. You will study how people have changed the places where they live.

You will also study the **culture** of people in different countries. Culture is the ideas, art, and way of life of a group of people. When you study about culture, you learn about food, clothing, sports, customs, and language of a group of people. **Religion** is also part of culture. Religion is the different ways people believe and pray to a god or to many gods. Culture

Brazil's leaders meet in these buildings in Brasília. This capital city is only about 50 years old.

Brasília, the capital of Brazil

is what makes one group of people different from another.

The Five Themes of Geography

We use five **themes**, or important ideas, to help us study different places. These five themes help us answer important questions about different parts of the world. The five themes of geography are: **location**, **place**, **human/environment interaction**, **movement**, and **region**. You will use the five themes again and again as you study world geography.

Let's look at each of the themes:

Location: This theme helps us answer the question, "Where is the place?" Sometimes the answer to this question describes what a place is near. The location of a place might be near a river, a mountain, or a city. For example, Brasília, the capital city of Brazil, is 600 miles from the Atlantic Ocean. It is near a smaller city called Anápolis. Think about the place where you live. How would you describe its location?

Sometimes we need to find the exact spot on a map or a globe where a place can be found. To find the exact location of a place, we use lines of **latitude** and lines of **longitude**. Lines of latitude are lines on a map that go from east to west. Lines of longitude are lines that go from north to south. Every place on Earth has its own latitude and longitude. The exact location of Brasília is 16° south latitude and 48° west longitude. No other place on Earth is at that same location.

Place: This theme helps us answer the question, "What makes this place different from all other places on Earth?" A place may be different because of its culture. Brasília is a special place because it was built to be Brazil's new capital city almost fifty years ago. All of the city's buildings look modern. Also, it was built in an area that had few people. Today Brasília is a big city with almost two million people. For these reasons, there is no other place like Brasília.

A place can also be different because of its **landforms**. A landform is the shape of an area on Earth's surface. Mountains, hills, plains, and **plateaus** are the four main kinds of landforms. Plateaus are high, flat land. Think about where you live. What makes it different from every other place?

Human/Environment Interaction: This theme answers the questions, "How do people use and work with the place? How do they change the place?" This theme tells how people can change a place. It also tells how people are changed by a place. By building Brasília, the people of Brazil changed that part of their country. It changed from a quiet area with few people to a large city with many government workers. Before the city was built, there was little transportation in that area. New roads, highways, and an airport were built to connect the new city to other parts of Brazil.

This theme also tells us how people change the way they live and work because of the place. For example,

Mountains are a kind of landform.

LANDFORMS

Plateau

Mountains

Hills

Plain

Shown here are four types of landforms. Which landforms can be found where you live?

People often change the place where they live. These trees were cut down to make a road to Brasília.

This ship will move goods from one country to another.

people who live near an ocean or a lake often earn a living by fishing. In places where gold and silver can be found, many people become miners. Think about where you live. How have people used, changed, and worked with your community's land and water?

Movement: This theme helps us answer the question, "How and why do people, goods, and ideas move from place to place?" Every year millions of people move from one place to another. After Brasília was built, government leaders moved to the new city. Then many other people moved there. They started businesses such as restaurants and stores. More people moved there, and the city grew larger.

Trade is the movement of goods from and to different places. Cars and clothes are made in many different countries. Ships and trains bring them to our country. Goods made in our country are shipped to other countries, too.

Culture also moves from one country to another. Americans were the first to wear denim jeans. Today people around the world wear the same kind of jeans that Americans wear. Think about where you live. Which people and goods have moved in and out of your community?

Region: To study Earth, people divide it into areas called regions. A region is an area in which the people or places share something important. Brasília is in the region that has Brazil's government. The city has government buildings and homes for government leaders. Often a region is described by its landforms. For example, a region may be covered with tall mountains. Places in a region may share the same climate. Sometimes the people in a region share the same culture. In what region is your community located?

Oceans and Continents

As you study world geography, you will learn about Earth's oceans and **continents**. A continent is a large body of land. Most of Earth is covered with water. Much of the water is in four large oceans. The oceans

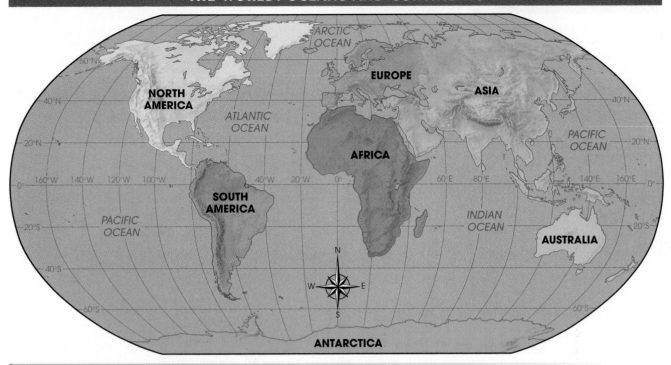

Most of Earth is covered with water. Most of Earth's land is found on seven continents. What are the names of the largest ocean and the largest continent?

in order of size from largest to smallest are the Pacific Ocean, the Atlantic Ocean, the Indian Ocean, and the Arctic Ocean.

Most of Earth's land is found on seven continents. The seven continents from largest to smallest are Asia, Africa, North America, South America, Antarctica, Europe, and Australia. On which of these continents is your home?

As you study world geography, you will learn about different regions and countries. Think about the ways each place is different or the same as your community.

Chapter Main Ideas

1. Geography is the study of the planet Earth.
2. The five themes of geography are location, place, human/environment interaction, movement, and region.
3. Earth has four oceans and seven continents.

◆ Vocabulary

Match Up Finish the sentences in Group A with words from Group B. Write the letter of each correct answer on the blank line.

Group A

Group B

1. A _____ is the ideas, art, and way of life of a group of people.

    A. region

    B. culture

2. The geography theme of _____ tells where to find a place.

    C. human/environment interaction

3. A _____ is a large body of land.

    D. continent

4. A _____ is an area that shares something important.

    E. location

5. The theme of _____ tells how people use and change a place.

◆ Read and Remember

Write the Answer Write one or more sentences to answer each question.

1. What are the five themes of geography? _____

_____

_____

2. How is Brasília different from all other places? _____

_____

3. How has movement changed the area of Brasília? _____

_____

4. What are the names of the four oceans? _____

_____

UNIT 1

The United States and Canada

Rocky Mountains

Niagara Falls

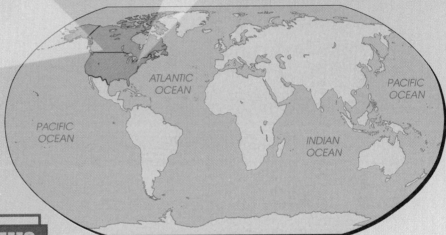

ATLANTIC OCEAN

PACIFIC OCEAN

PACIFIC OCEAN

INDIAN OCEAN

DID YOU KNOW?

▲ The name of Canada comes from *Kanata*, an American Indian word which means "village."

▲ Almost half of the fruits and vegetables grown in the United States come from California.

▲ It rains up to 350 days per year at Mt. Waialeale, Hawaii.

▲ In 1969 a dam was built to stop the water from flowing over the American side of Niagara Falls for a short time.

WRITE A TRAVELOGUE

Imagine you are a world traveler. You will be visiting the places described in this first unit. Keep a travelogue or a journal about your trip. Before reading Unit 1, write a paragraph about the places in the United States and Canada you would want to visit. After reading Unit 1, write a paragraph about two interesting places in these countries.

THEME: PLACE

CHAPTER 1

Two Nations of North America

Where Can You Find?

Where can you find the tallest place in North America?

Think About As You Read

1. What landforms are found in the United States and Canada?
2. Compare the climates of the United States and Canada.
3. How are the United States and Canada alike and different?

New Words

- official languages
- coastal plain
- mountain chain
- climates
- immigrants
- freedom of religion
- democracies
- urban
- suburbs
- industrial nations
- standard of living
- developed nations
- unguarded border

People and Places

- United States
- Canada
- Rocky Mountains
- Mount McKinley
- Alaska
- Great Lakes
- Arctic
- Hawaii
- Native Americans
- American Indians
- Spain
- France
- Great Britain
- Spanish
- French
- British

Two friends are visiting a large shopping mall in North America. The sound of rock music can be heard in many of the stores. Some of these stores sell jeans and sweatshirts. Other stores sell toys, telephones, or books. The two friends buy hamburgers for lunch.

Can you tell if this mall is in the United States or in Canada? It may be difficult to tell because both nations are alike in many ways. The signs in the mall can give you the answer. The signs in this mall are in both English and French. Both English and French are the **official languages** of Canada. The United States does not have an official language. Most people in the United States speak English as their main language.

Understanding the Land and the Climate

The United States and Canada are the two largest countries in North America. Canada is the world's second largest country in size. The United States is

CANADA AND THE UNITED STATES

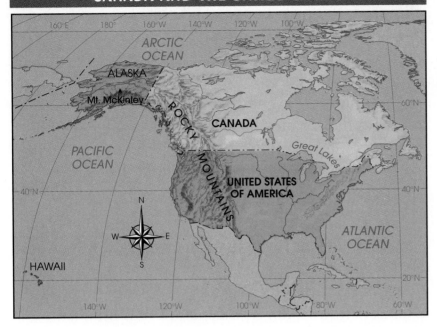

Canada and the United States share some of the same landforms. What mountain chain can be found in both countries?

the fourth largest country in the world. Find the United States and Canada on the map above.

The United States and Canada are between two large oceans. The Atlantic Ocean is to the east of both nations. The Pacific Ocean is to the west. The icy Arctic Ocean is north of Canada. The Atlantic and Pacific oceans help both nations. Both countries use the oceans for fishing. They use the oceans for trading with countries around the world.

The United States and Canada have the same kind of landforms. In the east both have a **coastal plain** along the Atlantic Ocean. A coastal plain is flat land near an ocean. Low mountains are to the west of the coastal plain. The tall Rocky Mountains are in the west. This **mountain chain** is 3,000 miles long. A mountain chain is a long group of mountains. One of these mountains, Mount McKinley in Alaska, is the tallest mountain in North America. Large plains are between the Rocky Mountains and the mountains in the east. These plains have good farmland.

Both countries have many large lakes. Four of the five Great Lakes are shared by the United States and Canada. The Great Lakes are among the largest lakes in the world.

Mount McKinley, Alaska

The Arctic in northern Canada is a very cold place to live.

Immigrants arrive in the United States.

The two countries have many different kinds of **climates**. Northern Canada and northern Alaska are in a region called the Arctic. This region is always very cold. Most of southern Canada has warm summers and very cold winters.

The United States has many different climates. Many northern states have long, cold winters and hot summers. Hawaii and some western and southern states have warm weather throughout the year.

History, People, and Government

For thousands of years, Native Americans, or American Indians, lived in many parts of North and South America. About 500 years ago, people from Europe began to settle in North and South America. Explorers from Spain, France, and Great Britain claimed large parts of North America. Spanish people settled in what is now the southern and western parts of the United States. Much of what is now Canada was settled by French people. British people settled in the eastern part of what is now the United States.

The French and the British fought against each other to rule more land in North America. They fought several wars. Finally, in 1763 the British won. After that, Great Britain ruled Canada. Many British people moved to Canada. Canada belonged to Great Britain until 1931. Today Canada rules itself.

Great Britain had ruled the eastern part of what is now the United States. In 1776 Americans decided to be free from Great Britain's rule. They fought and won a war for freedom. They called their new nation the United States of America.

For hundreds of years, **immigrants** have settled in the United States and in Canada. People from every part of the world now live in these countries. People in both countries have a lot of freedom. All people have the freedom to speak and to write as they wish. There is **freedom of religion** for all. This means people can pray any way they choose.

The United States and Canada are **democracies**. In a democracy, people vote for their leaders. They

Most people in Canada and in the United States live in urban areas. This city is in Canada.

also vote for their lawmakers. But the two countries are two different types of democracies. They have different types of governments. They have different laws and different kinds of leaders. You will read about their governments later in this unit.

Living in the United States and Canada

The United States and Canada are both large nations. However, the United States has ten times more people. In both nations most people live in cities, or **urban** areas. Many people live in areas close to the cities called **suburbs**.

In both nations only a small part of the people are farmers. But these farmers grow far more food than the people of their countries need. Both countries sell food to people in other countries.

The United States and Canada are **industrial nations**. An industrial nation has many factories. Both countries make cars, computers, and many other products. Most people in the United States and Canada have a high **standard of living**. The standard of living measures how well people live in a region. Both countries have plenty of businesses, schools, and hospitals. In both countries most people can afford to own cars, refrigerators, and telephones. A country that has few people who can afford to own these types of goods has a low standard of living.

Car parts are made in this factory in Canada.

The United States and Canada are friendly neighbors. Teams from the United States and Canada play each other in baseball, hockey, basketball, and other sports.

Both the United States and Canada are called **developed nations**. Developed nations are industrial nations with a high standard of living.

Both countries have a lot of trade with other nations around the world. The United States has more trade with Canada than with any other nation. Canada has more trade with the United States than with any other country.

There is real friendship between the two large nations of North America. The two countries share the world's longest **unguarded border**. There are no soldiers along an unguarded border. In the next chapters, you will learn more about the United States and Canada.

Chapter Main Ideas

1. The United States and Canada have the same kind of landforms. There are many different climates in both countries.
2. The United States and Canada are democracies. But they have different types of governments.
3. The United States and Canada are developed countries. Both are industrial nations with a high standard of living.

◆ Vocabulary

Finish Up Choose the word or words in dark print that best complete each sentence. Write the word or words on the correct blank line.

developed nation   **standard of living**   **democracy**
suburbs   **coastal plain**

1. A country that has people that choose their own leaders and write their

own laws is a _____.

2. A _____ has many factories, banks, and stores.

3. When a nation has a high _____, most people can afford to own cars, televisions, and telephones.

4. Communities near cities are called _____.

5. Flat land near an ocean is a _____.

◆ Read and Remember

Matching Each item in Group B tells about an item in Group A. Write the letter of each item in Group B next to the correct answer in Group A.

Group A

_____ **1.** Hawaii

_____ **2.** industrial nation

_____ **3.** Arctic

_____ **4.** French and English

_____ **5.** Great Britain

Group B

A. This type of nation makes many cars, planes, and computers in its factories.

B. This state in the United States is always warm.

C. This region in northern Canada is always very cold.

D. This nation once ruled Canada.

E. These are Canada's official languages.

Compare and Contrast   Read each phrase below. Decide whether it tells about Canada or the United States. If it tells about either nation, write the number of the phrase in the correct part of the Venn diagram. If the phrase tells about both nations, write the number of the phrase in the center of the diagram. The first one is done for you.

1. industrial nation

2. two official languages

3. many immigrants

4. fought Great Britain for freedom

5. warm climate throughout the year in south

6. democracy

7. second largest country in the world

8. no official language

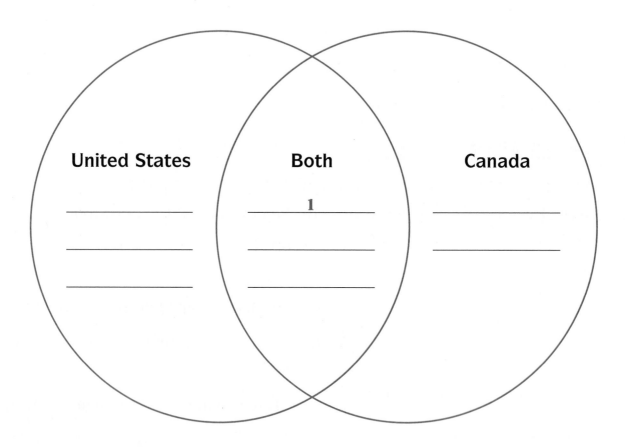

United States

Both

1

Canada

◆ **Journal Writing**

There are many ways that the United States and Canada are alike and different. Write a paragraph in your journal that tells at least one way the two countries are alike. Then tell one way they are different.

CHAPTER 2

The United States: Land of Variety

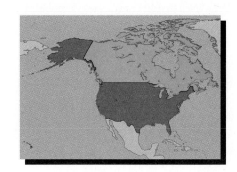

Where Can You Find?
Where can you find the hottest place in the United States?

Think About As You Read

1. How are the four regions of the United States different from each other?
2. What are some natural resources of the United States?
3. What are some problems of the United States?

New Words

- variety
- citizens
- natural resources
- population density
- cash crops
- technology
- service jobs

People and Places

- Puerto Rico
- New York City
- Los Angeles
- Chicago
- Washington, D.C.
- Northeast
- Midwest
- Great Plains
- Texas
- Oklahoma
- Mississippi River
- Gulf of Mexico
- Death Valley
- Africans
- African Americans
- Shannon Lucid

What do you want to do during your next winter vacation? Do you want to go swimming at a warm beach? Do you want to ski down a mountain? Do you want to see a play in a big city? In the United States, you could do all of these things and many more. The United States is a land of great **variety**.

Many States and Cities

In Chapter 1 you read that in 1776 Americans decided to be free from Great Britain. When the United States first became a free nation, it had only 13 states. Soon more states became part of the country. Today the United States is made up of 50 states. In 1959 Alaska became the forty-ninth state. Later that year Hawaii became the fiftieth state. These two states are far from all the other states. Alaska is north and west of Canada. Hawaii is a group of islands in the Pacific Ocean. The people in all 50 states are **citizens** of the United States. A citizen is a member of a country.

Flag of the United States of America

THE UNITED STATES OF AMERICA

CANADA

WA
MT ND MN WI MI
OR ID SD VT ME
WY IA Chicago NH MA
CA NV NE IL IN OH NY PA CT RI
UT CO New York City
Los DEATH KS MO KY WV VA NJ ATLANTIC
Angeles VALLEY TN NC MD DE OCEAN
AZ NM OK AR SC Washington D.C.
MS AL GA
TX LA
FL

ROCKY MOUNTAINS
Great Lakes
Mississippi River
PACIFIC OCEAN
Gulf of Mexico
MEXICO
AK
HI
PUERTO RICO (U.S.)

MAP KEY
- • City
- ⊛ Capital city
- –·– Border between countries
- —— State border

The Capitol in Washington, D.C.

Some parts of the United States are not states. One of these places is Puerto Rico. This island belongs to the United States. Puerto Rico is not a state. But the people of Puerto Rico are citizens of the United States.

There are many large cities throughout the United States. New York City, Los Angeles, and Chicago are the largest cities in the United States. Millions of people live in these cities. Millions more live in the suburbs close to the nation's cities. Washington, D.C., is the capital of the United States. The leaders of the United States work in Washington, D.C.

Regions of the United States

We can divide the United States into regions in order to study it. Let us look at four large regions—the Northeast, the Midwest, the South, and the West.

The first region is the Northeast. Its landforms are coastal plains and low mountains. It has many harbors. The Northeast region has fewer **natural resources** than other regions. Natural resources are things we get from Earth. Coal, fish, and forests are the most important natural resources of the Northeast.

The Northeast has many large cities. This region has the nation's highest **population density**.

This means that more people live closer together in this region than in any other part of the country. Many people work in factory jobs. There are also many people who work at fishing and trading.

The second region is the Midwest. It is near the Great Lakes. This region has coal and iron. There are many factories in the cities next to the Great Lakes. The factories use coal and iron to make cars and machines. Ships on the Great Lakes carry these products to many places.

The Midwest has huge flat plains. Some of these plains are called the Great Plains. Wheat is grown in this region. Bread, cereal, and flour are made from wheat. This region also has many dairy farms.

The South is the third region. Many people are moving to the South from other parts of the country. This region has a large coastal plain. It also has low mountains. Its warm climate is good for farming. Farmers grow **cash crops**, or crops they can sell. Some cash crops are cotton, rice, and oranges.

Oil is an important natural resource in states such as Texas and Oklahoma. Oil is made into many products such as gasoline for cars and planes.

The Mississippi River runs through many states in the Midwest and the South. The Mississippi starts in the Midwest in the north near Canada. The river is more than 2,000 miles long. It ends in the South at the Gulf of Mexico. Many rivers flow into the Mississippi.

The fourth region is the West. This is a region with many contrasts. The tall Rocky Mountains are in this region. The lowest place in all of North and South America is also in this region. It is Death Valley. Death Valley is the hottest place in the United States. The West has plains and valleys with good farmland. Many fruits and vegetables are grown in the valleys of the West. But there are also dry deserts in the West.

The West has many natural resources. Alaska has large amounts of oil. Many workers cut down trees in the forests in the West. Other people in the region work at mining or fishing.

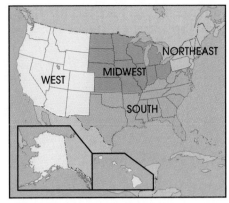
Four Regions of the United States

Death Valley

Americans use new technology to make many products.

How Do Americans Earn a Living?

There are many ways for Americans to earn a living. The land, the climate, and the natural resources of a region help people decide what kind of work to do. Farmers are a small part of the population. Many people work at factory jobs. Factories use new **technology** to make many new products. Technology is the inventions that improve the ways we live and work. Each year Americans build better cars, computers, and machines.

Most Americans now work at **service jobs**. Service jobs are jobs in which people help other people. People who work in schools, hospitals, banks, and stores are doing service jobs. People who work for the government have service jobs.

People who work as teachers have service jobs.

People of the United States

The United States has always been a country with people from many nations. The first Americans, the Indians, continue to live in many parts of the country. People from Europe were the first to move to America from other lands. Now most immigrants come from Asia, South America, and parts of North America.

In 1619 the first Africans were brought to America. Later more and more Africans were forced to be slaves in America. Slavery ended more than 130 years ago. Today more than 30 million African Americans live in the United States.

Today there are many different groups of people in the United States. They follow different religions. Some of them speak different languages. Each year thousands of new immigrants move to America. Some come to get better jobs. Many others come to have more freedom.

Looking at the Future

The United States is a strong, rich country. It is strong because it has a large army. It is also strong because it has good laws and good leaders. The government of the United States is a democracy. The leader of the country is the President. People vote every four years for a President. The people also vote for their lawmakers. The lawmakers meet in a group called Congress.

The United States is a rich country because it has so many natural resources, businesses, and factories. Excellent transportation has helped the country become rich. There are good highways, airports, and railroads. People and goods are able to move to all parts of the country.

Today the country does not have enough natural resources. Americans must now buy a lot of oil from other countries. Americans must work harder to save their own natural resources for the future.

The United States has very good highways. These roads help move goods around the country.

Lawmakers meet in a group called Congress. Here the President speaks to the people in Congress.

The United States is a rich country. But millions of Americans are poor. Some people do not have enough food. Other people do not have homes. Americans must find new ways to help the poor.

The United States tries to help other countries. It gives money and food to other countries. Americans work to bring peace to places that have wars. In the future the United States will continue to help other countries. And it will continue to be a land of variety.

Chapter Main Ideas

1. The United States is a land of variety. It has many different landforms, natural resources, and jobs.
2. The United States has four large regions. They are the Northeast, Midwest, South, and West.
3. People from many countries live in the United States. Many people move to the United States to have more freedom.

BIOGRAPHY

Shannon Lucid (Born 1943)

As a young girl, Shannon Lucid had a dream. She wanted to explore space. Through hard work her dream came true.

After she finished college, Lucid became a pilot. Later she studied to be an astronaut. She flew on several space trips. Then, in 1996 Lucid made history. She spent 188 days in space. During that time she worked for the United States on the Russian space station *Mir*. While in space she did many science experiments. She also exercised to keep her body strong. During the months in space, she did not see her family or friends. After six months Lucid returned to Earth. Americans everywhere were proud of Shannon Lucid. She had spent more time in space than any other American. From her work Americans have learned more about space travel.

Journal Writing
Write a paragraph in your journal that tells why Shannon Lucid is a hero to many Americans.

◆ Vocabulary

Finish the Paragraph   Use the words in dark print to finish the paragraph below. Write the words you choose on the correct blank lines.

cash crops   **natural resources**   **variety**
service jobs   **population density**

The United States is a land of _____ because it has many jobs,

landforms, and natural resources. The Northeast has a high _____

because many people live close together in this region. In the South farmers grow

_____, or crops they can sell. They grow cotton, rice, and oranges.

The West has many _____, or things we get from Earth. Most

Americans work at _____ where they help other people.

◆ Read and Remember

Complete the Chart   Use the facts from the chapter to complete the chart. You can read the chapter again to find facts you do not remember.

Regions of the United States

	Northeast	Midwest	South	West
What are the landforms?				
What are the natural resources?				
What work do people do?				

Matching   Each item in Group B tells about an item in Group A. Write the letter of each item in Group B next to the correct answer in Group A.

Group A

_____ **1.** Washington, D.C.

_____ **2.** Shannon Lucid

_____ **3.** Puerto Rico

_____ **4.** Oklahoma

Group B

A. This city is the capital of the United States.

B. The people of this island are citizens of the United States.

C. Oil is an important resource from this state.

D. This astronaut was in space for 188 days.

◆ Think and Apply

Categories   Read the words in each group. Decide how they are alike. Find the best title for each group from the words in dark print. Write the title on the line above each group. The first one is done for you.

American Democracy   **Landforms in the United States**
Natural Resources   **Largest Cities in the United States**

1. ___American Democracy___

vote for President
vote for lawmakers
freedom of religion

2. _____

New York City
Los Angeles
Chicago

3. _____

forests and fish
oil
gold, coal, silver, and iron

4. _____

Rocky Mountains
Great Plains
Death Valley

◆ Journal Writing

You read about four regions in this chapter. Write a paragraph in your journal that tells which region you might want to live in. Give two or more reasons why you chose this region.

Using Map Directions and a Compass Rose

There are four main directions. They are **north**, **south**, **east**, and **west**. There are also four in-between directions. They are **northeast**, **southeast**, **northwest**, **southwest**. A **compass rose** is used to show directions on a map. Sometimes the directions are shortened to **N**, **S**, **E**, and **W**. The in-between directions are shortened to **NE**, **SE**, **NW**, and **SW**.

A. Write the four main directions and the four in-between directions on the compass rose below. The first one is done for you

B. Look at the map of the United States below. Choose an answer from the box to finish each sentence. Use the compass rose to help you.

northwest	**northeast**
west	**north**
south	

1. The state of Maine is _____ of Louisiana.

2. The Gulf of Mexico is _____ of Louisiana.

3. The Great Lakes are _____ of Chicago.

4. The Pacific Ocean is _____ of California.

5. Oregon is _____ of New Mexico.

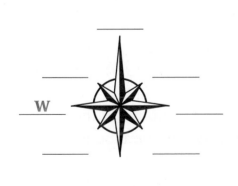

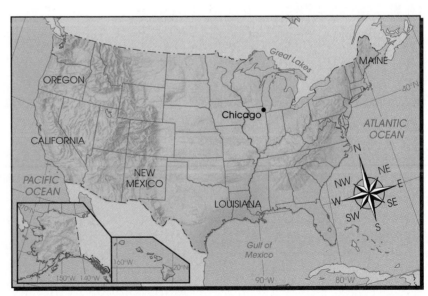

CHAPTER 3

Canada: A Giant Land of Few People

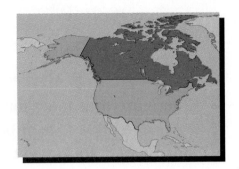

Where Can You Find?

Where can you find the oldest city in Canada?

Think About As You Read

1. Why do most Canadians live in the southern part of Canada?
2. What are some of Canada's regions?
3. What kind of government does Canada have?

New Words

- provinces
- territories
- permafrost
- logging
- newsprint
- lowlands
- waterways
- British Commonwealth
- prime minister
- Parliament

People and Places

- Canadian Shield
- Hudson Bay
- St. Lawrence Lowlands
- St. Lawrence River
- Toronto
- Montreal
- Ottawa
- Quebec City
- Vancouver
- First Nations
- Inuit
- Eskimos
- Northwest Territories
- Nunavut
- Quebec
- French Canadians

Perhaps one summer you will visit northern Canada. Although it may be summer, the air will feel cold. People will be wearing warm jackets. You might want to visit a big city. You will not find one. Few people live in this part of Canada. Most Canadians live in the warmer southern part of Canada.

Canada's Land, Climate, and Natural Resources

In many ways Canada seems like the United States. There are coastal plains and low mountains in the east. There are the tall Rocky Mountains in the west. There are large flat plains between the mountains. But Canada is different.

Canada is a very big country. It has ten states called **provinces**. Each province has its own government. To the north of the provinces are two **territories**. Many islands in the Arctic Ocean are part of these territories. Fewer than 100,000 people live in these two northern territories.

CANADA

MAP KEY
- City
- ⊛ Capital city
- - - - - New territory in 1999
- ——— Province border

Canada has ten provinces. In 1999 Canada will have a third territory. What is the name of the new territory?

Canada's flag

Canada has a small population. Only 28 million people live in this giant country. Most Canadians live within 200 miles of Canada's southern border. This area is warmer than northern Canada. In the summer the temperature in southern Canada is usually about 70°F. But in northern Canada it can be below 40°F. In most of Canada, the temperature during the winter is below 0°F.

The Arctic is the coldest part of northern Canada. Most of the year the ground is frozen. For a few weeks during the summer, the top layer of soil is not frozen. A few small plants can grow in this wet, muddy soil. But there are no trees here. Below the top layer of soil the ground remains frozen. **Permafrost** is the layer of soil that is always frozen. Crops cannot be grown where there is permafrost. But other parts of Canada have very good soil for growing crops.

Canada has many natural resources. Thick forests cover almost half of the country. Canada has a lot of oil and coal. It has gold, silver, iron, and other metals. There is also plenty of waterpower that is used to make electricity.

Parts of northern Canada are covered with snow during most of the year.

What Are Some of Canada's Regions?

The Canadian Shield is a large region that curves around Hudson Bay. Find the Canadian Shield on the map on page 25. The Canadian Shield covers almost half of Canada. Few people live in this cold region. But the region is very important because it has many forests and natural resources. Many people in this region work at **logging**. Logging means cutting down trees in the forests. One important forest product is **newsprint**. Newsprint is the paper used for making newspapers. Canada makes more newsprint than any other country.

Southeast of the Canadian Shield is a narrow region called the St. Lawrence Lowlands. **Lowlands** are low, flat land. The St. Lawrence River is in this region. The Great Lakes and the St. Lawrence River are Canada's busiest **waterways**. Ships carry products through the Great Lakes, to the St. Lawrence River, and then to the Atlantic Ocean. More than half of Canada's people live in the St. Lawrence Lowlands. Toronto and Montreal, Canada's largest cities, are in this region. Canada's capital, Ottawa, is also in this region. Quebec City, the oldest city in Canada, is here, too. It was started by the French in 1608.

The western part of Canada includes the Great Plains and the Rocky Mountains. Wheat is an important

Newspapers being printed on newsprint

The logging industry is found in many parts of Canada. This truck is at a logging site in western Canada.

Wood from Canada's forests is shipped from Vancouver to other countries.

crop on Canada's Great Plains. There are many farms in this region. In some areas people raise cattle. Canada, like the United States, has cowboys to take care of the cattle. Canada's busiest port, Vancouver, is in the west. Vancouver is warmer than Canada's eastern cities. Its water never freezes, so ships use this port all year. From Vancouver, Canada sends goods across the Pacific Ocean.

History, People, and Government

The Indians were the first people to live in Canada. Indian groups are called First Nations in Canada. Then about 5,000 years ago, Inuit people settled in northern Canada. Inuit are also called Eskimos. For thousands of years, Inuit have lived in the Arctic. In the past Inuit hunted and fished for their food. They traveled using dogsleds. Now they travel using snowmobiles and cars. Today Inuit work in mining and oil industries.

An Inuit pilot

Most Inuit live in the eastern part of the Northwest Territories. In 1999 this area will become a new territory called Nunavut. The remaining western part will still be called the Northwest Territories.

In Chapter 1 you read how the French and the British settled Canada. The French were the first people from Europe to settle in Canada. They first

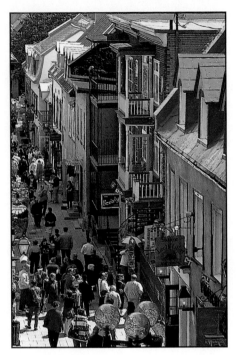

Quebec City

Great Britain's queen, who is also Canada's queen, visits Canada.

settled in the area of Quebec City. Today almost one third of Canada's people are French Canadians. Most of them live in the province of Quebec.

In 1763 the British won control of Canada from the French. Canada became free from Great Britain in 1931. There continues to be a strong friendship between Canada and Great Britain. Canada is part of the **British Commonwealth**. It is a group of nations that were once ruled by Great Britain. Great Britain's queen is also Canada's queen. Almost half of Canada's people are from families that came from Great Britain. Canada also has immigrants from many other nations.

Canada is a democracy. The leader of Canada is the **prime minister**. The people of Canada vote to choose their lawmakers. The lawmakers work in a group called **Parliament**.

Looking at Canada's Future

Many people in Canada care more about their own province than about their country. This is a very big problem in Quebec. Many French Canadians want Quebec to be a separate country. In 1995 people in Quebec voted about separating from Canada. There were enough votes for Quebec to remain part of Canada. But the people of Quebec may vote about separating from Canada again. Canadians must work together to keep Quebec part of their country.

Canada is an important country. It is a rich nation with many resources. Canada works at helping poorer nations. It also sends soldiers to keep peace in other countries. In the years ahead, Canada will continue to be an important country.

Chapter Main Ideas

1. Most Canadians live in southern Canada. Northern Canada is too cold for farms, factories, or cities.
2. The Canadian Shield is a cold region with few people but great natural resources.
3. Canada is a democracy. A prime minister leads the country. Laws are made by Parliament.

Montreal

Imagine being in a French city with 3 million people. The street signs are in French. In many schools the teachers speak only French. But this French city is not in France. It is in the province of Quebec in Canada. The city is Montreal. It is the second largest French city in the world.

Montreal is located on an island. The island is in the St. Lawrence River. It is in southern Quebec. The city was built around a mountain. Montreal is located in the St. Lawrence Lowlands region.

Montreal has the world's largest underground shopping center. The shopping center has more than 200 stores and restaurants. People can go shopping even on the coldest, snowiest days.

Montreal has one of the world's finest subway systems. Trains move quickly under the city's streets. The trains are quiet because they have rubber tires. There is much beautiful artwork in the subway stations. The people of Montreal can enjoy looking at art as they ride to work.

Write a sentence to answer each question.

1. Location   Where is Montreal?

_____

2. Region   In which region is Montreal?

_____

3. Movement   What do people in Montreal use to travel around the city?

_____

USING WHAT YOU'VE LEARNED

◆ Vocabulary

Analogies   An **analogy** compares two pairs of words. The words in the first pair are alike in the same way as the second pair. Use the words in dark print that best complete the sentences.

waterway   logging   province   prime minister   permafrost

1. State is to California as _____ is to Quebec.

2. Sand is to the desert as _____ is to the Arctic.

3. President is to the United States as _____ is to Canada.

4. Road is to car as _____ is to ship.

5. Mining is to metals as _____ is to forests.

◆ Read and Remember

Where Am I?   Read each sentence. Then look at the words in dark print for the name of the place for each sentence. Write the name of the correct place on the blank after each sentence.

Vancouver   Canadian Shield   St. Lawrence Lowlands
Nunavut   Ottawa

1. "I am in an area where most of the Inuit live."_____

2. "I am in the capital of Canada."_____

3. "I am in western Canada in the country's busiest port."_____

4. "I am in the region that has the cities of Toronto, Montreal, and Quebec."

_____

5. "I am in a cold, rocky region with few people and many natural resources."

_____

Write the Answer   Write one or more sentences to answer each question.

1. What is the population of Canada?_____

2. What is permafrost?_____

_____

3. What are some of Canada's natural resources?_____

_____

4. Who is Canada's queen?_____

_____

5. Which province voted to remain in Canada in 1995?_____

_____

◆ Think and Apply

Sequencing   Write the numbers **1, 2, 3, 4,** and **5** next to these sentences to show the correct order. The first one is done for you.

_____   Canada became free from Great Britain in 1931.

_____   The French explored and settled in North America.

_____   People in Quebec voted to remain part of Canada.

_____   Great Britain won control of Canada from the French.

___1___   The Inuit first settled in the Arctic.

◆ Journal Writing

Think about the different regions in Canada. Choose the one region where you might want to live. Write a paragraph in your journal that tells why you would want to live in that region.

SKILL BUILDER

Reading a Map Key

Maps often use **symbols**, or little pictures, to show information. A **map key** tells what the symbols mean.

A. Look at the map key in the map below. Then write what each symbol means on the blank next to the symbol.

1. 〜 _____

2. ✲ _____

3. ★ _____

4. — _____

5. • _____

6. ▲ _____

B. Study the map key and the map of Canada below. Then write the answer to each question.

1. In what province is the capital of

   Canada? _____

2. What mountain peak is in the Yukon

   Territory? _____

3. Name two cities on the Great Lakes.

   _____ and

   _____

4. What is the capital of the province of

   Alberta? _____

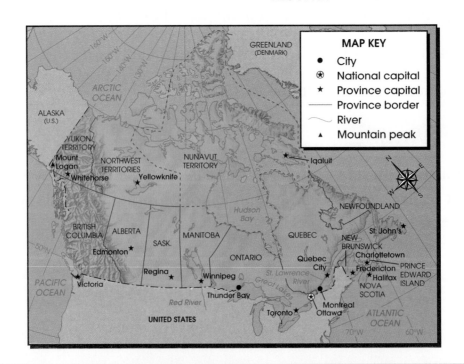

CHAPTER 4

The United States and Canada Work Together

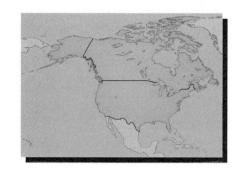

Where Can You Find?
Where can you find a 450-mile waterway that is shared by Canada and the United States?

Think About As You Read

1. How can NAFTA help trade?
2. What are some problems between the United States and Canada?
3. How has the St. Lawrence Seaway helped both countries?

New Words

- ◆ exports
- ◆ imports
- ◆ manufactured goods
- ◆ NAFTA
- ◆ tariffs
- ◆ pollution
- ◆ acid rain
- ◆ canals

People and Places

- ◆ Mexico
- ◆ Lake Erie
- ◆ St. Lawrence Seaway

Each year American and Canadian sports teams play many games against each other. Baseball, hockey, and soccer are a few of the sports that build friendship between the two countries.

Trade and NAFTA

Trade is important between the United States and Canada. Each country has more trade with the other than with any other country.

Canada **exports**, or sells to other countries, many products including cars, machines, oil, newsprint, wood, and wheat. Canada **imports**, or buys from other countries, a variety of items. Canada imports fruits, vegetables, and **manufactured goods** from the United States. Manufactured goods are goods that are made in factories.

The United States exports food, machines, cars, and other products to many nations. The United States imports cars, cameras, oil, and other products from

Leaders from Canada, the United States, and Mexico signed the North American Free Trade Agreement, or NAFTA.

President Clinton signed NAFTA in 1993.

other nations. The United States buys many products from Canada.

To improve trade, the United States, Canada, and Mexico signed a trade agreement in 1993. It is called **NAFTA**, or the North American Free Trade Agreement. This agreement helps trade because with NAFTA there are fewer **tariffs**. A tariff is a tax that is paid on imported goods. Tariffs make imported goods more expensive. For example, Canada might put a tariff on shoes that were made in the United States. Then the American shoes would cost more in Canada than shoes that were made in Canada. So Canadians would not buy the American shoes. Tariffs make people want to buy cheaper goods that are made in their own countries. By the year 2005, there will be few tariffs on goods traded between the United States, Canada, and Mexico. Then there will be free trade among the three countries.

NAFTA will make it easier for workers in one country to get jobs in the other countries. It will be easier for each country to start businesses in the other countries. Not everyone likes NAFTA. Some people are afraid that businesses will move from their own country to another country. If businesses move away, many people could lose their jobs. Most people hope that NAFTA will help businesses in all three countries.

Problems Between Neighbors

You learned that Canada is an industrial nation. But many of its factories and businesses are owned by American companies. Many Canadians are not happy that Americans control so many of their businesses.

Many Canadians believe there is too much American culture in their country. Canadians watch American television shows and movies. They listen to American music. But Canadians want their people to pay more attention to their own culture. They also want Americans to learn more about Canada's culture.

Another problem is **pollution**. Pollution means that the air and the water are not clean. Both nations have many cars and factories. These cars and factories send smoke and dirt into the air. This causes air pollution. They also send dirt and chemicals into the water. This causes water pollution. Water pollution hurts fish and plants that live in lakes, rivers, and oceans.

Pollution has hurt the Great Lakes. It did the most harm to Lake Erie. Fish could no longer live in its water. The United States and Canada have worked together to clean the water in the Great Lakes. Both countries passed laws to protect the Great Lakes. The water in Lake Erie is now much cleaner. But still some of the fish in the Great Lakes are not safe to eat.

The two nations are working together to end the problem of **acid rain**. Acid rain forms when pollution in the air becomes part of the rain. Pollution from American factories has caused acid rain in Canada. Canadians are angry because acid rain has killed fish in lakes and rivers. It has killed trees and plants in forests. To stop acid rain, both countries have passed clean air laws. American cars and factories now send much less pollution into the air.

Americans and Canadians Work Together

In 1954 the United States and Canada began building the St. Lawrence Seaway together. The

Pollution in Lake Erie

This leaf shows what happens because of acid rain.

This ship is passing through one of the canals of the St. Lawrence Seaway.

The International Peace Garden is on the border between the United States and Canada.

Seaway is a group of **canals** that go through the rocky part of the St. Lawrence River. The Seaway makes it possible for large ships to sail through the Great Lakes and down the St. Lawrence River. Then ships can sail into the Atlantic Ocean. The trip through the Seaway is about 450 miles long. Ships from many nations use the Seaway to trade with the United States and Canada. Waterpower from the Seaway is used to make electricity. This electricity is used by cities in both nations. The St. Lawrence Seaway has helped both countries.

The United States and Canada share a strong friendship. They also share a long unguarded border. A beautiful peace garden on the border brings people from both countries together.

Chapter Main Ideas

1. The United States and Canada have more trade with each other than with any other country.
2. The United States and Canada are working together to stop air and water pollution and acid rain.
3. The United States and Canada built the St. Lawrence Seaway together. Both countries use electricity from the Seaway.

◆ Vocabulary

Find the Meaning Write the word or words that best complete each sentence.

1. To **import** goods means to _____ another country.

   sell them to   buy them from   share them with

2. Two kinds of **manufactured goods** are _____.

   apples and corn   water and soil   cars and telephones

3. **Tariffs** make goods from other countries _____.

   cheaper   stronger   more expensive

4. A **canal** is a _____.

   road for cars   track for trains   waterway for ships

5. **Acid rain** forms when rain mixes with _____.

   pollution   snow   mud

◆ Read and Remember

Finish the Paragraph Use the words in dark print to finish the paragraph below. Write the words you choose on the correct blank lines.

   Mexico   **Great Lakes**   **imports**   **sports teams**   **tariffs**

The United States and Canada work together. They have _____ that play against each other. Both nations have a lot of trade with each other. NAFTA will end most _____ between the United States, Canada, and _____. People in these countries want NAFTA to help trade. The United States _____ many products from Canada. Both nations are working to end pollution in the _____.

Find the Main Idea   A **main idea** is an important idea in a chapter.
Less important ideas support the main idea. Read the five sentences below.
Choose the main idea and write it in the main idea box. Then find three
sentences that support the main idea. Write them in the boxes of the main
idea chart. There will be one sentence in the group that you will not use.

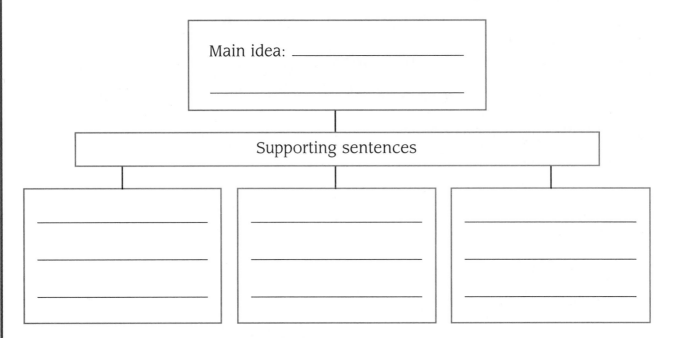

Main idea: _____

_____

Supporting sentences

a. Canada exports wheat and oil.

b. The United States and Canada work together in many ways.

c. Both nations have passed laws to stop pollution.

d. The United States and Canada built the St. Lawrence Seaway together.

e. Both nations are working to stop acid rain.

◆ **Journal Writing**

Imagine you are a newspaper reporter. Write a paragraph that tells about
the problems caused by acid rain and pollution. Write at least one way that
the United States and Canada are working together to solve the problems.

Latin America

Mexico City

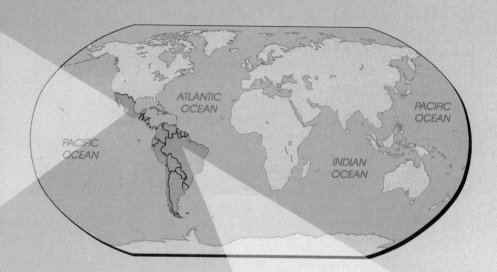

ATLANTIC OCEAN

PACIFIC OCEAN

PACIFIC OCEAN

INDIAN OCEAN

DID YOU KNOW?

▲ The Amazon River has enough water to fill a million bathtubs.

▲ There are hundreds of volcanoes in Central America.

▲ More than 40 ships pass through the Panama Canal every day.

▲ More than 6 million people from the United States and Canada visit Mexico each year.

▲ Most American baseballs are made in Haiti.

▲ Long ago, the Aztec Indians in Mexico played a game that was like basketball.

Amazon River

WRITE A TRAVELOGUE

In this unit you will be visiting many places in Latin America. Keep a travelogue about your trip through this region. Before reading Unit 2, write a paragraph that describes the places in the photographs above. After reading Unit 2, write three or more paragraphs that describe how Latin America is a region.

THEME: REGION

CHAPTER 5

Land and People of Latin America

Where Can You Find?
Where can you find the longest river in Latin America?

Think About As You Read

1. What kinds of landforms and climates are in Latin America?
2. What kinds of people live in Latin America?
3. How do people earn a living in Latin America?

New Words

- Latin
- tropics
- Equator
- Northern Hemisphere
- Southern Hemisphere
- tropical climate
- tropical rain forest
- elevation
- sea level
- mestizos
- developing nations
- subsistence farmers
- plantations

People and Places

- Latin America
- Caribbean Sea
- Middle America
- Central America
- Andes Mountains
- Amazon River
- Portugal
- Catholics
- Venezuela

Which part of the world has the longest mountain chain? Which region has the most Spanish-speaking people? From where in the world do we get most of our coffee and bananas? The answer to all of these questions is Latin America.

Landforms of Latin America

Latin America includes all of the nations south of the United States. This region is called Latin America because most people speak Spanish or Portuguese. Both of these languages developed from **Latin**. Latin is a very old language that few people speak today.

Find Latin America on the map on page 41. Latin America has three parts. The islands in the Caribbean Sea form one part. Middle America is another part. This part includes Mexico and the countries of Central

Mountains cover large areas of Latin America. What large mountain chain can be found in South America?

America. The third and largest part is the continent of South America.

Mountains cover large areas of Latin America. Some of these mountains are volcanoes. The tall Andes Mountains are in the west of South America. The Andes mountain chain is the longest one in the world. Plains and plateaus cover other parts of Latin America.

There are important rivers in South America. The longest river in South America is the Amazon River. Other large rivers join the Amazon. Many people use these rivers for transportation.

The Tropics

Most of Latin America is in a region called the **tropics**. This is a hot region near the **Equator**. The Equator is an imaginary line that divides the globe in half. The halves are called the **Northern Hemisphere** and the **Southern Hemisphere**. The Equator is the line of latitude that is 0°. The plains near the Equator have a **tropical climate**. A tropical climate is hot all

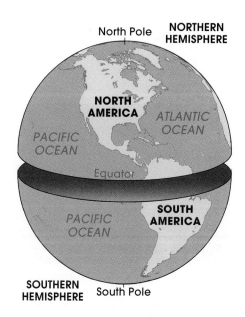

The Equator divides Earth into the Northern Hemisphere and the Southern Hemisphere.

These mountains in the tropics are always covered with snow.

An Indian weaver in Central America

the time. It is hot because this region receives more direct sunlight for a longer period of time than other parts of the world. It is also very rainy in the tropics.

Latin America has the world's largest **tropical rain forest**. These thick forests are found near the Equator. They grow where the climate is very hot and very wet. The largest tropical rain forest is in South America. Smaller tropical rain forests can be found in Middle America and on islands in the Caribbean Sea.

Many parts of Latin America have cooler climates even though they are in the tropics. This is because of their **elevation**. Elevation tells you how high the land is above **sea level**. The climate becomes colder as the land's elevation gets higher. Some very tall mountains in the tropics are always covered with snow.

There are two other reasons why some parts of Latin America have cooler climates. First, the southern part of South America is very far from the Equator. As you move away from the Equator, the climate becomes colder. The second reason is that ocean winds give the coastal plains and the islands in the Caribbean Sea milder climates.

History, People, and Culture

Indians were the first people to live in Latin America. Five groups of Indians built great nations in Latin America. They built good roads and large cities.

Five hundred years ago people from Spain conquered most of Latin America. They forced Indians to be their slaves. Millions of Indians died while working for the Spanish. Then the Spanish brought slaves from Africa to work in Latin America.

Spain ruled most of Latin America. But Portugal ruled the huge nation of Brazil. Other countries in Europe also ruled smaller colonies.

In the early 1800s, Latin Americans fought to rule themselves. By 1826 most countries were free.

Who are the people of Latin America today? Some are white people whose families came from Europe. Some people are Indians. Most people are **mestizos**. A mestizo is a person who has European and Indian ancestors. There are also many black people in the Caribbean countries and in Brazil.

The Spanish culture is important in most of Latin America. People in most countries speak Spanish. The Spanish brought the Catholic religion to the region. Today most Latin Americans are Catholics.

Almost three fourths of the people in Latin America live in cities. Some of the world's largest cities are in Latin America. Most of the cities are found on the plateaus and the coastal plains of Latin America. It is hard to live in tall mountains or in tropical rain forests. So these areas of Latin America have small populations.

A Catholic church in Mexico

Earning a Living

Most countries in Latin America are **developing nations**. A developing nation is a nation with a low standard of living and not much industry. In the cities most people work at service jobs. Some people work in factories. Many people in Latin America are farmers.

There are two kinds of farmers in Latin America. There are poor **subsistence farmers** who work on small farms. They try to grow enough food for their families. The second kind of farmer grows cash crops. Coffee, bananas, and sugarcane are important cash crops in Latin America. Cash crops are grown on huge farms called **plantations**. A very small part of the

Subsistence farmers will usually only grow enough food to feed their families. Any extra crops will be sold in a local market.

Latin America has many natural resources. This iron mine is near the Amazon River.

Mine workers in South America

population owns most of the plantations. Millions of poor farmers work on the plantations.

Latin America has many natural resources. Some countries have metals such as silver and copper. In these countries many people work in mines. A few countries like Mexico and Venezuela have oil. But there is little iron and coal in Latin America. These two resources are needed to make cars, trucks, and other machines. This is one reason why there is not much industry in Latin America.

In the next chapters, you will learn more about the land, people, natural resources, and problems of different nations in Latin America. You will find out what people in these nations are doing to solve their problems.

Chapter Main Ideas

1. Many parts of Latin America are covered with mountains and tropical rain forests. The tropical rain forests grow where the climate is very hot and wet.
2. Most people in Latin America speak Spanish and follow the Catholic religion.
3. Most countries in Latin America are developing nations. Many people in Latin America are farmers.

◆ Vocabulary

Match Up Finish the sentences in Group A with words from Group B. Write the letter of each correct answer on the blank line.

Group A

1. The _____ is half of the globe.

2. A _____ has European and Indian ancestors.

3. _____ grow only enough food for their families.

4. _____ means how high the land is above sea level.

5. The hot region of Earth near the Equator is

the _____ .

Group B

A. Subsistence farmers

B. tropics

C. Elevation

D. Northern Hemisphere

E. mestizo

◆ Read and Remember

Finish Up Choose the word or words in dark print that best complete each sentence. Write the word or words on the correct blank line.

Amazon   **tropical**   **bananas**   **Spanish**   **Andes**

1. In most Latin American countries, people speak _____ .

2. The world's longest mountain chain is the _____ .

3. The longest river in South America is the _____ .

4. A _____ climate is hot all the time.

5. Coffee, sugarcane, and _____ are important cash crops in Latin America.

Drawing Conclusions Read the first two sentences below. Then read the third sentence. Notice how it follows from the first two sentences. The third sentence is called a **conclusion**.

> There are mountains in Middle America.
> There are mountains in South America.

Conclusion: Many parts of Latin America have mountains.

Read each pair of sentences. Then look in the box for the conclusion you might make. Write the letter of the conclusion on the blank. The first one is done for you.

1. Tall mountains near the Equator are covered with snow.
   Ocean winds cool the islands in the Caribbean Sea.

   Conclusion: __C__

2. The first people in Latin America were Indians.
   Later, people from Europe and Africa came to Latin America.

   Conclusion: _____

3. Many people in Latin America have a low standard of living.
   Most countries in Latin America do not have much industry.

   Conclusion: _____

4. Most people in Latin America speak Spanish.
   Most people in Latin America are Catholics.

   Conclusion: _____

Conclusions
   A. There are many kinds of people in Latin America.
   B. The Spanish brought their language and religion to Latin America.
   C. Some parts of the tropics have cooler climates.
   D. Many nations in Latin America are developing nations.

◆ **Journal Writing**

Write a paragraph in your journal that tells about landforms, rivers, and tropical rain forests of Latin America.

CHAPTER 6

Mexico: A Nation of Contrasts

Where Can You Find?
Where can you find the largest city in the world?

Think About As You Read

1. What landforms and climates are found in Mexico?
2. How is Mexico becoming an industrial nation?
3. What contrasts can be seen in Mexico?

New Words

- tourists
- colony
- traditional
- tortillas
- rural
- slums
- upper class
- lower class
- middle class
- national debt
- illegal immigrants
- illegal drugs

People and Places

- Rio Grande
- Acapulco
- Central Plateau
- Mexico City
- Aztec
- Father Miguel Hidalgo
- Tenochtitlan

Each winter thousands of Americans leave their cold cities to travel to Mexico's warm beaches. These **tourists** enjoy the many contrasts found in Mexico.

Mexico's Landforms and Climates

Mexico shares its long northern border with the United States. A river called the Rio Grande is part of this border. Mexico has two long coasts with sandy beaches. The beaches of Acapulco are on the Pacific coast. The Gulf of Mexico is to the east.

Tall mountain chains are in the eastern and western parts of the country. Between the two mountain chains is the large Central Plateau. The Central Plateau has a mild climate because of its high elevation. In the north the plateau does not receive much rain. The land is mostly used for cattle ranches. In the south there is more rain and better soil. Many farms are in the south. Part of southern Mexico has a tropical climate. Tropical rain forests are found in this part of Mexico.

Mexico is located between the Pacific Ocean and the Gulf of Mexico. What three countries share borders with Mexico?

MEXICO

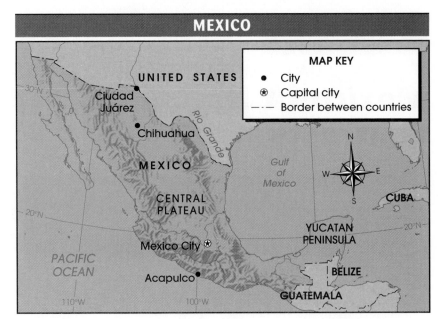

Mexico's flag

Father Miguel Hidalgo

Most of Mexico's people live on the Central Plateau. Most Mexicans live in cities. Mexico City is the nation's capital. It is the largest city in the world. About twenty million people live in and around Mexico City.

Mexico's History, People, and Culture

Hundreds of years ago, Indians built great nations on the land that is now Mexico. One Indian nation, the Aztec, built schools, temples, and beautiful cities. The Spanish conquered and destroyed the Aztec. Then the Spanish built a **colony** in Mexico. A colony is land that is ruled by another nation.

In the early 1800s, Mexico became the first Spanish colony to fight to be free. Father Miguel Hidalgo started the fight for freedom. By 1821 Mexico was a free country. But Mexicans continued to fight among themselves to control their country.

In the 1840s, Mexico and the United States fought against each other. The United States wanted Mexican land. Mexico lost the wars. Mexican land to the north of the Rio Grande became part of the United States.

Today Mexico is a democracy. A president leads the nation. Mexico also has a congress.

Who are the people of Mexico today? More than half of the people are mestizos. More than one fourth are Indians. There are also white people whose families once came from Europe.

Spanish and Indian cultures have mixed together to form a Mexican culture. There are many **traditional** villages where people speak Indian languages. Many Indians also speak Spanish. The Spanish language and the Catholic religion are part of Mexico's culture. Mexico is the world's largest Spanish-speaking nation. Mexicans love to watch bullfights. They enjoy spicy foods made with peppers. Mexicans make a special flat bread called **tortillas**, which are made from corn.

Making tortillas

A Developing Nation

Mexico is one of the three nations that signed NAFTA. This trade agreement has helped Mexico sell more products to the United States. It has helped many American companies build new factories in Mexico. The workers in the factories are Mexicans. These factories are helping Mexico become an industrial nation. Mexico is trying to become a developed nation.

Oil is Mexico's most important resource. Mexico also has coal, iron, and silver. Mexico mines more silver than any other country. Mexico earns money by exporting oil and minerals. It sells oil to the United States and to other countries.

Mexico also makes money from tourists. Tourists spend about 4 billion dollars in Mexico each year.

Only a small part of Mexico's land is good for farming. Most of the farmland is used to grow corn. Corn is the main food used by Mexicans. Some cash crops are grown on larger farms. Mexico earns money by exporting cash crops such as sugarcane, wheat, oranges, tomatoes, and bananas.

In **rural** areas of Mexico, most people are poor farmers. Rural areas are places that are not near cities. Most rural people are subsistence farmers. They grow corn, beans, rice, and squash for their families. Most subsistence farmers have a low standard of living. Many families do not own a car or have a telephone. People may use animals for farm work and for traveling.

Every day many poor people move to Mexico City and to other cities to find better jobs. Millions of poor

Tourists in Mexico

Mexico City is the largest city in the world.

people live in **slums** that surround these cities. They live in small, poorly made homes.

As in other Latin American countries, most of Mexico's land, businesses, and money are owned by a small group of wealthy people. These rich people are called the **upper class**. The rich people live in large, beautiful homes. Most people in Mexico are poor and belong to the **lower class**. Mexico has a small **middle class** that is not rich or poor. The middle class is slowly growing larger in Mexico.

Solving Problems for the Future

One of Mexico's biggest problems is a huge **national debt**. A country's national debt is the money that it has borrowed and must repay. This problem became very serious in Mexico in 1995. Mexico had borrowed billions of dollars from other countries. But in 1995, Mexico did not have enough money to pay its debts. The United States helped Mexico by lending the country billions of dollars. That money helped Mexico. In 1997 Mexico paid back all the money it had borrowed from the United States.

Each year many poor Mexicans move to the United States. Most have permission to move to the United States. But some Mexicans are **illegal immigrants**. They are people who move to the United States without permission from the American

Millions of poor people are living in slums in Mexico City.

Many small villages can be found in the hills of southern Mexico.

government. The United States wants Mexico to stop illegal immigrants from entering the United States.

Each year millions of dollars of **illegal drugs** come to the United States from Mexico. It is against the law to sell these drugs in the United States. The United States wants Mexico to work harder to stop illegal drugs from coming into the country.

Mexico is a nation of contrasts. There are contrasts in the landforms and the climate. There are contrasts between modern cities and rural farms. Mexicans are working to improve the standard of living for all of the people of Mexico.

Chapter Main Ideas

1. Most Mexican cities and people are on the Central Plateau.
2. Mexico has many new factories and is trying to become an industrial nation.
3. A large contrast between rich and poor can be seen in Mexico.

Illegal immigrants crossing the border between Mexico and the United States

Mexico City

Imagine living in a city that is more than a mile high. It is surrounded by mountains that are so tall they are always covered with snow. This mile-high city is Mexico City. It is Mexico's capital. It is on the Central Plateau of Mexico. The city has about twenty million people. It is the largest city in the world. It is also the center of Mexico's industry, government, culture, and transportation.

Mexico City first began in the 1300s. At that time the Aztec Indians built a city on the place that is now Mexico City. They built their beautiful city, Tenochtitlan, on an island in a lake. They built bridges to connect their city to the mainland. In 1512 the Spanish conquered the Aztec. They destroyed the Aztec city. The Spanish removed all the water from the lake and built a new city where the Aztec city had been. The new city, Mexico City, became Mexico's capital.

Today Mexico City is very crowded. Poor people from all over Mexico move to Mexico City each day. It also has become a place with terrible air pollution. The city's cars and factories cause pollution. The tall mountains that surround the city prevent the dirty air from moving away from Mexico City. It is no longer healthy to breathe the air in this beautiful capital.

Pollution in Mexico City

Write a sentence to answer each question.

1. Location   What is Mexico City's location?

_____

2. Movement   How has the movement of people changed Mexico City?

_____

3. Human/Environment Interaction   Why does Mexico City have pollution problems?

_____

◆ Vocabulary

Forming Word Groups   Read each heading on the chart below. Then read each word in the vocabulary list on the left. Form groups of words by writing each vocabulary word under the correct heading. You should use one answer twice. The first one is done for you.

Vocabulary List		
upper class		
lower class		
illegal drugs		
tourists		
illegal immigrants		
middle class		
city slums		

Understanding Mexico

Types of People	Mexico's Problems
1. _middle class_	1. _____
2. _____	2. _____
3. _____	3. _____
4. _____	
5. _____	

◆ Read and Remember

Find the Answer   Put a check (✔) next to each sentence that tells about a problem in Mexico. You should check four sentences.

_____ **1.** Mexico has a huge national debt.

_____ **2.** There are millions of poor people.

_____ **3.** Many tourists go to Acapulco in the winter.

_____ **4.** Many illegal immigrants go to the United States.

_____ **5.** Mexico is the largest Spanish-speaking nation.

_____ **6.** Illegal drugs are sent from Mexico to the United States.

_____ **7.** Mexico shares its long northern border with the United States.

◆ Think and Apply

Cause and Effect   A **cause** is something that makes something else happen. What happens is called the **effect**.

> **Cause:**   Many Mexicans in rural areas need jobs.
> **Effect:**   They move to cities to find work.

Match each cause on the left with an effect on the right. Write the letter of the effect on the correct blank. The first one is done for you.

Cause

1. Mexico's beaches are warm during the winter, so __D__.

2. The southern part of the Central Plateau has good soil, so _____.

3. The Spanish conquered the Indians of Mexico, so _____.

4. Mexico has lots of oil, so _____.

5. The United States won wars against Mexico, so _____.

6. Some Mexicans are rich but most are poor, so _____.

Effect

A. it sells oil to other countries

B. land north of the Rio Grande became part of the United States

C. most farms are in the south

D. many tourists visit Mexico

E. there is a small middle class

F. their cultures have mixed together to form a Mexican culture

◆ Journal Writing

Write a paragraph in your journal about a problem in Mexico today. Tell how you think the problem could be solved.

Using a Distance Scale

A **distance scale** compares distance on a map with distance in the real world. We use a distance scale to find the distance between two places. Many distance scales show distance in both miles and kilometers.

Look at the map of Mexico below. The distance scale tells us that 1 inch on the map is the same as 600 miles in Mexico. There is about 1 inch between the cities of Chihuahua and Matamoros on the map. So the real distance between the two cities is about 600 miles.

Draw a circle around the word or numbers that finish each sentence. Use a ruler to measure the distance scale and distances on the map.

1. There is about _____ between Matamoros and Acapulco.

   1/10 inch   1/2 inch   1 inch

2. Using the scale, we know that the distance between Matamoros and Acapulco is about _____ miles.

   5   125   600

3. There are almost _____ inches between Acapulco and Ciudad Juárez.

   1   2   10

4. Using the scale, we know that the distance between Acapulco and Ciudad Juárez is about _____ miles.

   100   600   1,050

5. The distance from Ciudad Juárez to Mexico City is about _____ miles.

   300   900   2,000

6. The distance from Chihuahua to Mexico City is about _____ miles.

   300   750   1,500

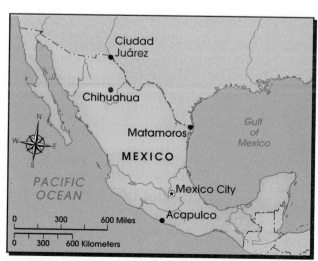

CHAPTER 7

Central America: Seven Countries in the Tropics

Where Can You Find?
Where can you find the only freshwater lake in the world that has sharks?

Think About As You Read

1. What are the important landforms of Central America?
2. Why has Nicaragua had civil wars?
3. How are Costa Rica and Panama different from other Central American nations?

New Words

- highlands
- lava
- earthquakes
- dictators
- civil war
- Communist
- inflation
- isthmus
- democratic

People and Places

- Maya
- Belize
- Guatemala
- Panama
- Nicaragua
- Lake Nicaragua
- Sandinistas
- Cuba
- Soviet Union
- El Salvador
- Honduras
- contras
- Violeta Barrios de Chamorro
- Costa Rica
- Panama Canal

Central America is smaller than the state of Texas. But this region has seven countries. In this chapter, you will learn about life in this region.

The Region of Central America

Central America is located between Mexico and South America. The Pacific Ocean is to the west. The Caribbean Sea is to the east. All seven nations are in the tropics. Find the names of the seven countries on the map on page 57.

Coastal plains are found in the east and the west of Central America. Most cities and plantations are in low mountains called **highlands**. Taller mountains cover a large part of Central America. Some of these mountains are dangerous volcanoes. When a volcano explodes, hot **lava**, or melted rock, pours onto the nearby land. Countries in Central America often have **earthquakes**. During an earthquake the ground shakes and often cracks open. Farms, cities, and

CENTRAL AMERICA

Map showing Central America with:

MAP KEY
- ⊛ Capital city
- — Canal
- –·– Border between countries

MEXICO, Belmopan, BELIZE, Guatemala City, GUATEMALA, HONDURAS, EL SALVADOR, San Salvador, Tegucigalpa, NICARAGUA, Managua, Lake Nicaragua, San José, COSTA RICA, PANAMA, Panama City, PANAMA CANAL, Caribbean Sea, PACIFIC OCEAN, SOUTH AMERICA

There are seven countries in Central America. Which country is located where Central America and South America meet?

people have been destroyed by volcanoes and earthquakes.

Most people in Central America earn a living through farming. Coffee, bananas, sugarcane, and cotton are the most important cash crops. Most cash crops are grown on large plantations. These plantations are owned by a few rich people. Most people in Central America are very poor. They work on plantations and earn very low salaries. Some people in the region work at mining minerals. Some people work in factories making cotton clothing.

Central America has a long history. More than 2,000 years ago, Indians called the Maya built great cities in this region. In the early 1500s, the Spanish conquered most of Central America. They ruled the region for 300 years. In 1821, six of the seven nations won their freedom from Spain. Belize was a British colony that became free in 1981.

There are different kinds of people in Central America. More than half of the people in Guatemala are Indians. In other countries most people are mestizos or white. There are many African Americans in Panama, Nicaragua, and Belize.

Looking at Nicaragua

Nicaragua is the largest country in Central America. Its landforms and climate are like those of the other

A volcano in Central America

Nicaragua's flag

nations in this region. Nicaragua earns most of its money by selling cotton, coffee, and sugarcane.

Lake Nicaragua is the country's largest lake. It is the only freshwater lake in the world with sharks. One of the islands in Lake Nicaragua has two volcanoes.

For many years **dictators** ruled Nicaragua. A dictator has full power to make laws. These dictators controlled the country's land and money.

Sandinista soldiers

During the 1970s, people called Sandinistas fought a **civil war** against the country's dictator. During a civil war, the people of the same country fight against each other. The Sandinistas won this civil war and took control of the government. The Sandinistas received help from Cuba and the Soviet Union. Those two nations were **Communist** countries and enemies of the United States. In a Communist country, the government controls all businesses. Sandinista soldiers also helped Communists fight in civil wars in El Salvador and Honduras.

The United States did not want Communists to have power in Central America. For a number of years, the United States gave money to people called contras. The contras were against the Sandinistas. The contras and the Sandinistas fought another civil war in Nicaragua. Finally, in 1990 the Sandinistas and the contras agreed to allow free elections in Nicaragua. The civil war ended.

Violeta Barrios de Chamorro

The people elected Violeta Barrios de Chamorro to be president. People voted for Chamorro because she was against the Sandinistas. But as president she allowed some Sandinistas to have power in the government.

Nicaragua has had many problems since its civil war ended. The long war destroyed many parts of the country. Many people do not have jobs. Most people earn very little money. **Inflation** is another big problem. Inflation means that food and goods become more and more expensive to buy. Inflation makes people need more money to buy almost everything.

These bananas were grown on a plantation in Costa Rica.

Costa Rica's flag

Peaceful Costa Rica

Costa Rica is south of Nicaragua. It is a peaceful country. It has never had a civil war. Costa Rica does not even have an army. Costa Rica is also different because its government is a strong democracy.

Costa Rica has the highest standard of living in Central America. Most people work on small farms, but they have a comfortable life. The country exports cash crops such as coffee and bananas. It also earns money from tourists. Costa Rica has more factories than other nations in the region. Factory workers make food products, clothing, machines, medicines, and other goods. The people of Costa Rica are proud of their peaceful democracy.

Panama and the Panama Canal

Panama is south of Costa Rica. It joins Central America to South America. Panama is an **isthmus** between the Atlantic and Pacific oceans. An isthmus is a narrow piece of land that is between two large bodies of water.

During the early 1900s, the United States built a canal across Panama. To build the Panama Canal, thousands of workers cut through mountains and rain forests. The Panama Canal allows ships to sail from the Atlantic Ocean through Panama to the Pacific

San José is Costa Rica's capital.

The Panama Canal saves weeks of travel time. By sailing through the Canal, ships do not have to go around South America.

Flag of Panama

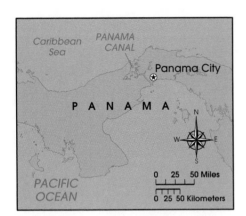

The Panama Canal

Ocean. Panama earns a lot of money from ships that use the Canal. The United States has controlled the Canal since it was built. But at the end of 1999, Panama will have control of the Canal.

Working for a Better Future

To help the people of this region, more people must own land. Once people own land, their government could help them get seeds and farm machines so they can be better farmers. The region also needs more industry so that countries in the region can sell more products other than cash crops.

Civil wars have been a big problem in many Central American nations. The nations of Central America need strong **democratic** governments. They also need peace. Peace will help all people of the region to have a better life.

Chapter Main Ideas

1. Large areas of Central America are covered with mountains. Most people live in highlands.
2. The Sandinistas lost the civil war in Nicaragua. The people elected a new president in 1990.
3. Costa Rica is a peaceful democracy. Costa Rica has the highest standard of living in Central America.

◆ Vocabulary

Finish the Paragraph   Use the words in dark print to finish the paragraph below. Write the words you choose on the correct blank lines.

dictator	**earthquakes**	**isthmus**
civil war	**highlands**	**inflation**

In Central America most people and cities are in the low mountains called

_____. This region sometimes has _____ in which

the ground shakes and cracks open. During a _____ the people of

the same country fight against each other. Before 1990 a _____

ruled Nicaragua and had full power to make laws. Food and goods in Nicaragua

continue to become more expensive. This problem is called _____.

Panama is an _____ because it is a narrow piece of land between

two large bodies of water.

◆ Read and Remember

Write the Answer   Write one or more sentences to answer each question.

1. How do most people in Central America earn money?

_____

2. What did the Maya do in Central America long ago?

_____

3. How did the civil war end in Nicaragua in 1990?

_____

4. What are two ways that Costa Rica is different from Nicaragua?

_____

♦ Think and Apply

Fact or Opinion A **fact** is a true statement. An **opinion** is a statement that tells what a person thinks.

> **Fact** Costa Rica does not have an army.
> **Opinion** Costa Rica should have an army.

Write **F** next to each fact below. Write **O** next to each opinion. You should find four sentences that are opinions.

_____ **1.** Coffee, bananas, sugarcane, and cotton are cash crops in Central America.

_____ **2.** Cash crops are grown on large plantations.

_____ **3.** Costa Rica has the highest standard of living in Central America.

_____ **4.** There are too many farmers in Central America.

_____ **5.** People should not live near the Panama Canal.

_____ **6.** Costa Rica is a democracy.

_____ **7.** Many people in Nicaragua do not have jobs.

_____ **8.** The Maya built better cities than the Aztec.

_____ **9.** The Panama Canal makes it easier for ships to sail from the Atlantic Ocean to the Pacific Ocean.

_____ **10.** The United States should keep control of the Panama Canal after 1999.

♦ Journal Writing

Write a paragraph in your journal that compares Nicaragua and Costa Rica. Tell how the two countries are alike. Tell how they are different.

Locating Places on a Grid

The map below is a **grid map** for part of Panama City, the capital of Panama. **Grids** are often drawn on maps to help find places on the map. Each place on the map is in a grid square. On this map the Museum is located in square B-2.

Look at the map below. Then answer each question.

1. What place is in square E-2?_____

2. What place is in B-3?_____

3. What road is in C-1?_____

4. In which grid square is the Supreme Court of Justice located? _____

5. What road is in B-4?_____

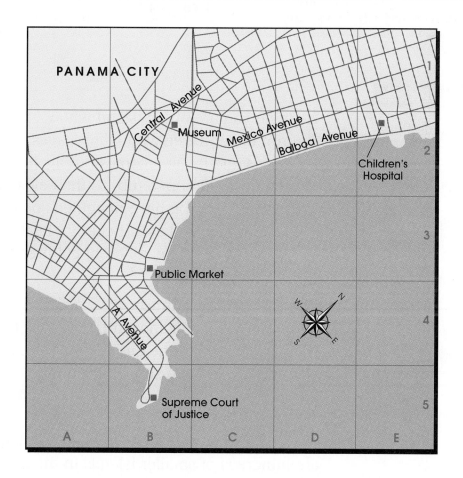

CHAPTER 8

The Caribbean: Hundreds of Beautiful Islands

Where Can You Find?
Where can you find the oldest city started in the Western Hemisphere by Europeans?

Think About As You Read

1. How do people in the Caribbean Islands earn a living?
2. In what ways have cultures mixed together in the Caribbean Islands?
3. In what ways are Cuba, Haiti, and the Dominican Republic alike? How are they different?

New Words

- ◆ tropical storms
- ◆ hurricanes
- ◆ tourism
- ◆ bauxite
- ◆ aluminum
- ◆ calypso
- ◆ independent
- ◆ Western Hemisphere
- ◆ Eastern Hemisphere

People and Places

- ◆ Caribbean Islands
- ◆ Greater Antilles
- ◆ Lesser Antilles
- ◆ Bahamas
- ◆ Jamaica
- ◆ Christopher Columbus
- ◆ Hispaniola
- ◆ Haiti
- ◆ Dominican Republic
- ◆ Fidel Castro
- ◆ Toussaint L'Ouverture
- ◆ Jean-Bertrand Aristide
- ◆ Santo Domingo

Imagine you are on an island when it begins to rain. You run under a tree with giant leaves. Soon the rain stops and the sun comes out again. There is a cool breeze. Workers return to the fields. More tourists arrive in a ship. You have imagined some parts of life on the Caribbean Islands. Beautiful beaches, large plantations, and many different cultures can be found on these islands.

The Caribbean Islands

The Caribbean Islands are located between the Atlantic Ocean and the Caribbean Sea. Look at the map on page 65. You can see that there are three groups of islands in this region—the Greater Antilles, the Lesser Antilles, and the Bahamas.

The Greater Antilles has four large islands. There are hundreds of smaller islands in the Lesser Antilles. Mountains cover many of these islands. Some of these

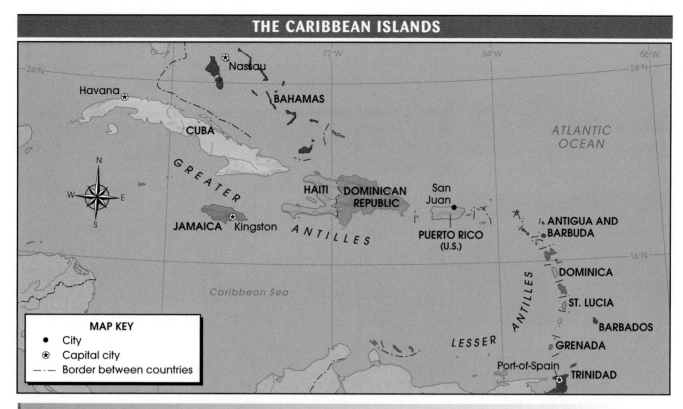

There are three groups of islands in the Caribbean region. The largest islands in the Caribbean are in the Greater Antilles. What is the largest island in this region?

mountains are volcanoes. The Bahamas and some of the Lesser Antilles islands are mostly flat.

Most of the Caribbean Islands are in the tropics. Cool winds from the sea keep the islands at about 80°F all year. **Tropical storms** are a problem between July and October. Tropical storms bring heavy rains and strong winds. The worst tropical storms are **hurricanes**. Hurricane winds can tear trees out of the ground and blow down houses. Rainfall during a hurricane often causes floods.

A hurricane passed through this Caribbean island.

Every year millions of tourists visit the Caribbean Islands. Many people work in service jobs in the **tourism** industry. They work in hotels, restaurants, and stores that tourists visit.

Most people in the Caribbean Islands work in farming. The Caribbean Islands earn most of their money from cash crops. Sugarcane is the most important cash crop. Bananas, oranges, rice, and pineapples are also exported. Most Caribbean Island countries have to import food for their people.

There is little industry in the Caribbean Islands. But some countries have factories where food products are made. In some countries, people work in mines. Many people in Jamaica work in **bauxite** mines. A metal called **aluminum** is made from bauxite.

The Culture of the Caribbean

Christopher Columbus explored the Caribbean for Spain. Later, Spain started colonies on several islands including Cuba, Puerto Rico, and Hispaniola. Other European countries also started colonies. They brought African slaves to work on plantations. Today most people in the Caribbean have ancestors who were brought to the islands from Africa.

Different cultures from Europe and Africa mixed together in the Caribbean Islands. For example, **calypso** music is a mix of African, Spanish, and American music. Today Spanish, French, English, and other languages are spoken on different islands. Some people speak Caribbean languages that use words from African and European languages.

Many Caribbean Islands are **independent** countries. Some islands do not rule themselves. For example, Puerto Rico is not independent. It belongs to the United States. Let's look at three Caribbean countries: Cuba, Haiti, and the Dominican Republic.

Cuba: A Communist Country

Cuba is close to the United States. It is only 90 miles from Florida. But the United States and Cuba are not

A calypso band

Many different languages can be heard in this marketplace in the Dominican Republic.

Sugarcane is cut by hand on this plantation in Cuba. Sugar is Cuba's most important export.

Flag of Cuba

friendly neighbors. They are enemies because Cuba is a Communist country. Cuba is the only Communist country in the **Western Hemisphere**. North America and South America are in the Western Hemisphere. Asia, Africa, Europe, and Australia are continents in the **Eastern Hemisphere**.

Before 1959 many businesses and sugarcane plantations in Cuba were owned by Americans. Many times the United States sent soldiers to Cuba to protect American businesses. Since 1959 a dictator named Fidel Castro has ruled Cuba. He started a Communist government in Cuba. Castro took control of all the American businesses and plantations in Cuba. They are now owned by Cuba's government.

Many Cubans were unhappy with Castro. About one million Cubans have moved to the United States. Others have moved to Mexico and Spain.

Today Cuba has many problems. Cuba gets little money from tourism. Cubans do not have enough food or money. But Castro has improved schools, roads, and health care.

Fidel Castro

Haiti and the Dominican Republic

Haiti is in the western part of Hispaniola. Haiti is covered with mountains. There is not much farmland. Most people in Haiti are poor farmers. Their farms are very small, so there is not enough food.

Haiti and the Dominican Republic are located on the island of Hispaniola.

Haiti began as a French colony. The French brought many African slaves to work on their plantations. In 1791 an African slave, Toussaint L'Ouverture, began a fight for freedom. Haiti became independent in 1804.

Haiti has been ruled by many dictators. Since 1990 Haiti has tried to become a democracy. The country held free elections. The people elected Jean-Bertrand Aristide to be president. Haiti's army forced the new president to leave. But in 1994 the United States sent soldiers to Haiti to help Aristide rule his country. In 1995 the people of Haiti voted for a new president.

The Dominican Republic is on the eastern part of Hispaniola. Its capital, Santo Domingo, is the oldest city started in the Western Hemisphere by Europeans. Spanish is the language of the Dominican Republic.

The Dominican Republic is larger than Haiti. It also has more farmland. Sugarcane is the main cash crop. This country is more developed than Haiti. There are more factories. The Dominican Republic also earns money from tourism.

The Future of the Caribbean Islands

All countries in the Caribbean Islands are developing nations. Too many people are poor farmers. These countries need to grow more food to feed their people. Most Caribbean countries depend too much on sugarcane to earn money. Sometimes the price of sugar drops. Then these countries cannot earn enough money. Millions of people do not have jobs. New industries will give more people jobs. The Caribbean is a beautiful region. But the people of this region need a higher standard of living.

Jean-Bertrand Aristide

Chapter Main Ideas

1. Different cultures from Europe and Africa mixed together in the Caribbean Islands. The people speak many languages and have different cultures.
2. Sugarcane is the most important cash crop on most Caribbean Islands. There is not much industry.
3. Cuba, Haiti, and the Dominican Republic are developing nations.

◆ Vocabulary

Analogies Use the words in dark print that best complete the sentences.

aluminum   **Western Hemisphere**   **hurricanes**   **calypso**

1. Sugarcane is to cash crop as _____ is to music.

2. Europe is to Eastern Hemisphere as North America is to _____.

3. Oranges are to orange juice as bauxite is to _____.

4. The Arctic is to snowstorms as the Caribbean is to _____.

◆ Read and Remember

Where Am I? Read each sentence. Then look at the words in dark print for the name of the place for each sentence. Write the name of the correct place on the blank after each sentence.

Dominican Republic   **Haiti**   **Puerto Rico**
Santo Domingo   **Cuba**   **Jamaica**

1. "I am in a country with many bauxite mines."_____

2. "I am in a place that belongs to the United States."_____

3. "I am in a Communist country, and it is 90 miles from Florida."

_____

4. "I am in a poor country that held free elections in 1990."_____

5. "I am in the oldest European city in the Western Hemisphere."

_____

6. "I am in a Spanish-speaking country that is in the eastern part of Hispaniola."

_____

Finish Up   Choose the word or words in dark print that best complete each sentence. Write the word or words on the correct blank line.

tourism	**tropical storms**	**Greater Antilles**
farming	**volcanoes**	**sugarcane**

1. There are four large islands in the _____.

2. Some of the mountains in the Caribbean Islands are _____.

3. Between July and October there are many _____ in the Caribbean.

4. Many people work in service jobs in the _____ industry.

5. Most people in the Caribbean Islands work in _____.

6. The most important cash crop in the Caribbean Islands is _____.

◆ Think and Apply

Sequencing   Write the numbers **1, 2, 3, 4,** and **5** next to the sentences below to show the correct order.

_____ In 1990 the people of Haiti elected Jean-Bertrand Aristide to be president.

_____ Fidel Castro became president of Cuba.

_____ Toussaint L'Ouverture led the fight for freedom in Haiti.

_____ Spain and other European countries started colonies in the Caribbean.

_____ The United States Army helped Jean-Bertrand Aristide return to Haiti to become president again.

◆ Journal Writing

Write a paragraph in your journal that compares Haiti and Cuba. Tell how they are alike and how they are different.

Understanding Lines of Latitude

You have read that the Equator is an imaginary line around the center of Earth. It runs east and west. There are many more lines that run east and west around Earth. These lines are called **lines of latitude**. Lines of latitude help us find places on maps and globes. They form part of a grid.

Each line of latitude is named with a number of **degrees**. The Equator is 0°. All other lines of latitude are north or south of the Equator. There are 90 lines of latitude in the Northern Hemisphere. The North Pole is 90° North, or 90°N. There are 90 lines of latitude in the Southern Hemisphere. The South Pole is 90° South, or 90°S.

Look at the map of Middle America and the Caribbean below. Then circle the correct answer to finish each sentence.

1. The latitude of Mexico City is about _____.

   15°S   20°N   80°N

2. The latitude of San José, Costa Rica, is _____.

   10°N   10°S   40°S

3. The latitude of Jamaica is about _____.

   30°N   18°N   8°S

4. A city with a latitude of 20°N is _____.

   Santiago   Ciudad Juárez

   Panama City

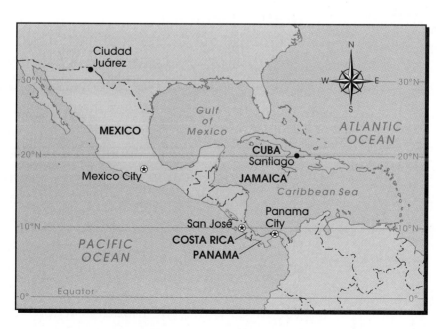

CHAPTER 9

Brazil: Home of the Amazon Rain Forest

Think About As You Read

1. How is Brazil different from other Latin American countries?
2. What is happening to the Amazon rain forest?
3. What kinds of products does Brazil export?

New Words

- ◆ mouth
- ◆ mulattos
- ◆ Carnaval
- ◆ interior
- ◆ basin
- ◆ deforestation
- ◆ oxygen
- ◆ poverty
- ◆ homeless

People and Places

- ◆ São Paulo
- ◆ Rio de Janeiro
- ◆ Brasília
- ◆ Amazon rain forest
- ◆ Amazon River basin
- ◆ Chico Mendes

Where can you find the longest river in the Western Hemisphere? Where can you find the world's largest rain forest? The answer to both questions is Brazil.

Brazil's Landforms

Brazil is the largest country in Latin America. Most of Brazil has a tropical climate. The world's largest tropical rain forest covers about half of Brazil. The Amazon River passes through this forest.

The Amazon is the world's second-longest river. It starts in the Andes Mountains in the western countries of South America. In Brazil the Amazon runs for more than 2,000 miles. Then it flows into the Atlantic Ocean. Ocean ships travel through Brazil on the Amazon. Many shorter rivers flow into the Amazon. The Amazon has a lot of water. In some places the river is several miles wide. The **mouth** of the Amazon is almost 100 miles wide. The mouth is where the river flows into the ocean.

BRAZIL

The Amazon River in Brazil is one of the world's longest rivers. What is the location of the mouth of the Amazon River?

Brazil's flag

Brazil has a wide coastal plain near the Atlantic Ocean. A large plateau covers the southern part of the country. This plateau has a milder climate than the northern part of Brazil. Most cities and farms are on the southern plateau.

Brazil's People, Cities, and Resources

Brazil has more people than any other country in Latin America. People from Portugal settled in Brazil in the 1500s. They brought the Catholic religion and the Portuguese language to Brazil. Today more than half of Brazil's people are white. There are also many black people and **mulattos**. A mulatto is a person with black and white ancestors. The Indian population in Brazil is small.

Most people in Brazil live within 200 miles of the Atlantic Ocean. Most of Brazil's people live in cities near the ocean. São Paulo is Brazil's largest city. It is one of the largest cities in the world.

Brazil is famous for its **Carnaval** holiday. During Carnaval people wear costumes and march and dance in parades. The most exciting Carnaval is in the city of Rio de Janeiro. Many tourists visit Rio for Carnaval.

Dancers in costume for Carnaval in Rio de Janeiro

From above, the rain forest looks like a thick, green blanket.

Brazil's government wants people to develop the western part of Brazil. This western region is called the **interior**. To develop the interior, Brazil built a new capital city there. You read about Brazil's capital, Brasília, in the introduction to this book.

Brazil has many natural resources. It has bauxite, gold, tin, iron, and other metals. There is waterpower for making electricity. Brazil also has some oil. But many natural resources are in the interior in the tropical rain forest. So they are hard to reach.

Brazil's Amazon Rain Forest

The Amazon rain forest covers about half of Brazil. It also covers parts of other South American countries. It is the world's largest rain forest. This forest is in the Amazon River **basin**. A basin is the area that drains into a river. Low plains surround the Amazon River.

What is it like to be in the rain forest? Thousands of different kinds of plants and animals live in the rain forest. Tall trees are everywhere. Some trees are hundreds of feet tall. Water drips off of the trees all the time because it rains so often. The ground is often wet and muddy. The climate in the tropics is hot. But the air in the rain forest feels cooler because the tall trees block the hot sun. Thick plants cover the ground where the sunlight shines through the tall trees. Plants need this sunlight to grow.

The Amazon rain forest is the largest one in the world. Many different types of plants and animals are found in this rain forest.

The rain forest has many resources. Nuts come from its trees. Rubber trees in the rain forest provide rubber for tires. Gold, tin, and other metals are in the earth. Medicines are made from trees and plants in the rain forest. No other part of the world has the trees and plants needed to make these medicines. These medicines help people who are very sick.

Deforestation

Brazil's rain forest is being destroyed. Destroying forests is called **deforestation**. Deforestation harms Earth's land, air, and water. People are cutting down trees to build roads through the forest. The new roads make it easier to travel through the region. People cut down the rain forest trees to mine metals and to have new farmland. After cutting the trees, they burn them in order to clear the land. There are now thousands of fires each day as more land is cleared. These fires cause terrible air pollution.

Trees in the rain forest are cut down to clear the land.

People have started farms and cattle ranches on cleared land. But the soil in the rain forest is not good for farming. It is also not good for raising cattle. After a few years, farmers cannot raise good crops on rain forest land. Then they move to another part of the rain forest. There they cut and burn more trees. They try again to farm the land. Each time this happens, more of the rain forest is destroyed. Most animals, plants, and trees of the rain forest can never be replaced. Small groups of Indians live in the rain forest. They use the rain forest, but they do not destroy it.

The rain forest is important to people in all parts of the world. Its trees send a gas called **oxygen** into the air. This oxygen makes the air cleaner and healthier to breathe. Many nations want Brazil to save its rain forest. People everywhere depend on oxygen and medicines from the rain forest.

Burning the rain forest

Working for a Better Future

Brazil is working to become a developed nation. Cars, machines, and shoes are a few of Brazil's factory products. Brazil exports factory goods and cash crops. Much of the world's coffee and sugar come from Brazil.

Homeless child in Rio de Janeiro

Poverty is a big problem in Brazil. Most plantation workers are poor. Slums surround Brazil's cities. Many children are **homeless**, or without homes. Brazil's government must find ways to help millions of poor people to have a higher standard of living.

The world is watching Brazil to see if it will save the Amazon rain forest. Brazil says it needs the forest's resources to help people earn more money. It is possible to get resources from the forest and not destroy it. By saving the rain forest, Brazil can use its resources to build a better future.

Chapter Main Ideas

1. Brazil is the largest country in Latin America.
2. People are destroying the Amazon rain forest in order to use its land and resources.
3. Brazil exports many factory goods and cash crops.

BIOGRAPHY

Chico Mendes (1944-1988)

Chico Mendes grew up in a poor family in Brazil. He became a leader among the rubber tappers in the Amazon rain forest. Rubber tappers remove rubber from rubber trees without harming the trees. Mendes became angry when people began chopping down rain forest trees. Rubber tappers could not work if the rubber trees were gone. So Mendes began his fight to save the rain forest.

Ranchers who wanted land in the Amazon rain forest hated Mendes. They said they would give him money if he stopped trying to save the trees. But Mendes continued his fight. He gave many speeches. People around the world learned why Brazil must save its rain forest.

On December 22, 1988, Mendes was killed in his own home by some ranchers. Other people are now doing the work Mendes started. They continue to fight for the Amazon rain forest.

Journal Writing
Write a paragraph in your journal that tells why Chico Mendes is a hero to many people.

◆ Vocabulary

Finish Up   Choose a word in dark print that best completes each sentence. Write the word on the correct blank line.

deforestation   oxygen   homeless   interior   basin

1. The western area of Brazil is the _____.

2. The area where water drains into a river is a river _____.

3. When a forest is destroyed, a region has _____.

4. We must breathe a gas in the air called _____.

5. People who do not have homes are _____.

◆ Read and Remember

Complete the Geography Organizer   Complete the geography organizer below with information about Brazil.

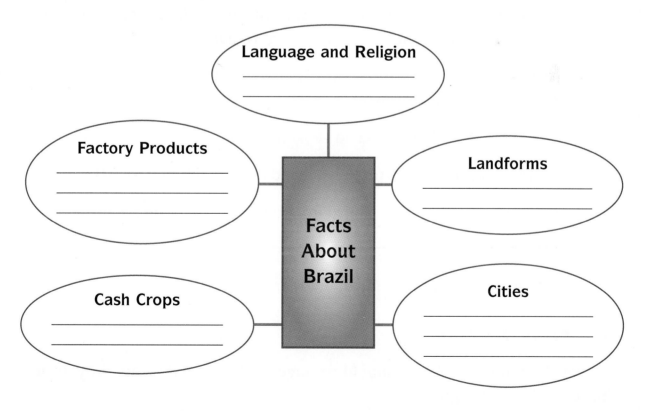

Matching   Each item in Group B tells about an item in Group A. Write the letter of each item in Group B next to the correct answer in Group A.

Group A

_____ **1.** Carnaval

_____ **2.** Amazon

_____ **3.** medicines

_____ **4.** farms and cattle ranches

_____ **5.** Brasília

Group B

A. This is the world's second longest river.

B. During this holiday, people wear costumes and dance in parades.

C. This capital city was built to help develop Brazil's interior.

D. The rain forest is being destroyed to make room for these.

E. These are made from trees and plants in the rain forest.

◆ Think and Apply

Finding Relevant Information   Information that is **relevant** is information that is important for what you want to say or write. Imagine you are telling your friend why it is important to save the Amazon rain forest. Read each sentence below. Decide which sentences are relevant to what you will say.

Put a check (✓) in front of the relevant sentences. The first one is done for you. Find two more relevant sentences.

___✓___ **1.** Trees in the rain forest send oxygen into the air.

_____ **2.** Medicines are made from plants and trees in the rain forest.

_____ **3.** Many minerals can be mined from below the rain forest's ground.

_____ **4.** Rain forests are located in the tropics.

_____ **5.** Indians need the rain forest in order to live.

◆ Journal Writing

Do you think the rain forest should be saved? Write a paragraph in your journal that explains your opinion.

Understanding Lines of Longitude

You learned that lines of latitude run east and west around Earth. There are also lines that run north and south around Earth. These lines are called **lines of longitude**. All lines of longitude meet at the North Pole and the South Pole. Lines of longitude are named with their number of degrees, just like lines of latitude. The **Prime Meridian** is a line of longitude that runs through Greenwich, England. The Prime Meridian is 0 degrees, or 0°. All other lines of longitude are east or west of the Prime Meridian. There are 180 lines of longitude to the west and 180 lines to the east.

Look at the map of Brazil below. Circle the answer to each question.

1. What is the longitude for São Paulo?

120°E   47°W   40°E

2. What is the longitude for Brasília?

48°W   148°E   10°E

3. What is the longitude of Manaus?

40°W   50°W   60°W

4. What city has the longitude of 35°W?

Manaus   Recife   Rio de Janeiro

5. How many large cities in Brazil are to the west of 60°W?

0   5   15

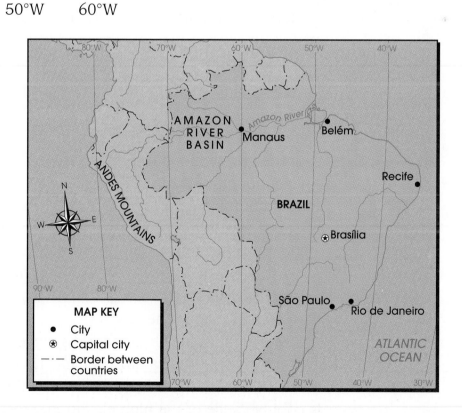

CHAPTER 10

The Countries of the Andes

Where Can You Find?
Where can you find the capital city with the highest elevation in the world?

Think About As You Read

1. What is the main landform of the Andean countries?
2. How does elevation change the climate in the Andes?
3. What problems are found in this region?

New Words

- empire
- Quechua
- coca
- cocaine
- drug traffickers
- terrorism
- terrorists
- ambassador
- marijuana

People and Places

- Andean countries
- La Paz
- Bolivia
- Peru
- Inca
- Lima
- Japan
- Colombia
- Alberto Fujimori
- Chile

Where can you find the world's longest mountain chain? Where can you find the world's longest country? The answer is in the countries of the Andes Mountains.

Landforms, People, and Climates of the Andes

There are five countries in the Andes Mountains. They are called the Andean countries. Find the five countries on the map on page 82. Look at how the Andes mountain chain is in all of these countries. These mountains are found along the west coast of South America. This mountain chain is more than 4,000 miles long.

Most of the people who live in the Andes Mountains are Indians, and some are mestizos. Most people are poor subsistence farmers.

The capital city with the world's highest elevation is in the Andes. It is La Paz, Bolivia. This capital is more than 12,000 feet high. The climate in La Paz is cool because of the high elevation. Most Andean

FOUR CLIMATE REGIONS IN THE ANDES

	Frozen Land, Tierra Helada (above 15,000 feet)
	Cold Land, Tierra Fria potatoes (7,000–15,000 feet)
	Mild Land, Tierra Templada coffee, corn, wheat (3,000–7,000 feet)
	Hot Land, Tierra Caliente sugarcane, coconuts, bananas (0–3,000 feet)
	Sea Level (0 feet)

The English and Spanish names for each region describe the region's climate. What crops grow in the Hot Land climate?

countries are in the tropics. Places in the tropics have hot, tropical climates. But in some parts of the Andean nations, the climate is not hot. The climate gets cooler as the elevation gets higher. The chart above shows four climate regions in the Andean countries.

Peru: The Largest Andean Country

Peru is the third largest country in South America. It is also the largest country in the Andes.

For thousands of years, Indians have lived in Peru. About the year 1200, the Inca Indians built a great **empire** in the Andes. An empire is an area where several nations are ruled by one nation. The Inca built cities and excellent roads. Their empire lasted more than 300 years.

The Spanish conquered the Inca in the 1500s. They built a Spanish colony in Peru. The Spanish built Peru's capital, Lima. It is on the coast. From Lima the Spanish sent Peru's minerals on ships to Spain.

In the 1820s Peru became free from Spain. Today Peru has two official languages. Spanish is one language. **Quechua**, an Indian language, is the other.

Today almost half of Peru's people are Indians. The Inca were their ancestors. Peru has the largest Indian population in South America. Many people in Peru are mestizos. Peru also has a small white population. There are some immigrants from Japan and other countries in Asia, too.

This is one of the places in Peru where the Inca once lived.

The Andes mountain chain is located along the length of western South America. In which countries are the Andes located?

MAP KEY
⊛ Capital city
– · – Border between countries

Farmer selling coca leaves

The small white population is Peru's upper class. The upper class owns most of Peru's land, businesses, and plantations. Most mestizos are in the lower class. They work on farms and in factories on the coastal plain. The Indians are the poorest people in Peru. Most are subsistence farmers. They raise potatoes, wheat, and corn in the mountains.

Many subsistence farmers grow a plant called **coca**. Coca is used to make an illegal drug called **cocaine**. In Peru and Colombia, people called **drug traffickers** pay the farmers to grow coca. Farmers earn more money from coca than from any other crop. Drug traffickers earn a lot of money by selling cocaine in the United States.

Peru has many natural resources. It has silver, tin, and other metals. There is also iron and oil. Many

Terrorists took over the home of Japan's ambassador to Peru.

minerals are found in the Andes. But they are hard to reach because they are in the mountains. Peru does not have enough good roads. It is hard to build roads through the Andes. The mountains make it difficult to travel from one place to another.

Terrorism is a very big problem in Peru. Terrorism is the use of dangerous acts against the people of a country. **Terrorists** try to destroy their enemies with these dangerous acts. In the 1980s and 1990s terrorists have tried to win control of Peru's government. They have killed about 30,000 people. In December 1996, terrorists forced hundreds of guests at the home of Japan's **ambassador** to be their prisoners. After four months, Peru's army was able to free the prisoners.

In 1990 Alberto Fujimori was elected president of Peru. He has tried to stop terrorism in Peru. He has also improved the country's economy. Peru had a terrible inflation problem. Peru's economy has been growing stronger. Many more people now work in factories and at jobs in cities. Inflation is not a problem in Peru today.

Alberto Fujimori

Chile: A Long, Narrow Country

Chile is south of Peru. It is more than 2,000 miles long. But it is only about 100 miles wide. The climate is colder in southern Chile than in northern Chile.

Most of Chile's cities and people are in a region called the central valley. The soil and climate are good for farming. Chile is in the Southern Hemisphere.

Coffee beans

When it is winter in the Northern Hemisphere, it is summer in the Southern Hemisphere. Chile's farmers grow fruits and vegetables during the summer. People in North America enjoy this summer fruit from Chile during the North's winter.

Colombia: Coffee Exports and More

Colombia is north of Peru. Colombia is the only country in South America with coasts on both the Pacific Ocean and the Caribbean Sea.

For many years most of Colombia's money came from exporting coffee. Now Colombia also has an oil industry. One day Colombia might earn more from oil than from coffee. Colombia also exports fresh flowers, bananas, and minerals.

Today people in Colombia earn more money from illegal drugs than from all other products. Drug traffickers are producing **marijuana** and cocaine. They sell these illegal drugs in the United States. Many crimes in Colombia and other countries are caused by these drug traffickers. The United States wants Colombia, Peru, and other countries to stop the work of drug traffickers.

The Future of the Andean Countries

The Andean countries have many poor people. Upper class people own most of the region's wealth. Governments must help the middle class grow larger.

The Indians of the Andes want the same rights and power as white people. Bolivia became the first country to elect a president who is an Indian. But most Indians still have fewer rights and less power.

The Andean countries need peace. They need peace from terrorists. They need peace from drug traffickers. Peace will help people work for a better future.

Chapter Main Ideas

1. The Andes Mountains are along the west coast of South America.
2. The Andean countries have four different climates because of elevation.
3. The Andean countries have had problems with inflation, terrorism, and drug traffickers.

Indians in Peru

◆ Vocabulary

Match Up   Finish the sentences in Group A with words from Group B. Write the letter of each correct answer on the blank line.

Group A

1. Peru has two official languages, Spanish and _____.

2. Many people have been killed by _____ who have used dangerous acts to try to win control of Peru.

3. The Inca built an _____ that lasted for 300 years.

4. In Colombia, people called _____ earn money from illegal drugs.

5. Two illegal drugs are cocaine and _____.

6. Subsistence farmers in Peru grow a plant called _____.

Group B

A. empire

B. marijuana

C. Quechua

D. drug traffickers

E. terrorists

F. coca

◆ Read and Remember

Write the Answer   Write one or more sentences to answer each question.

1. What mountain chain is found along the west coast of South America?

_____

2. What are the four climate regions of the Andes Mountains?

_____

3. Look at the map on page 82. What are the five Andean countries?

_____

4. What have terrorists done in Peru?

_____

5. What does the United States buy from Chile in the winter?

_____

6. What is the most important cash crop in Colombia?

_____

Find the Answer   Put a check (✔) next to each sentence that tells about a problem in the Andean countries. You should check three sentences.

_____ **1.** For thousands of years, Indians have lived in Peru.

_____ **2.** Drug traffickers sell illegal drugs from Peru and Colombia.

_____ **3.** It is very hard to build roads through the Andes Mountains.

_____ **4.** Fruits and vegetables grown in Chile are sold in the United States.

_____ **5.** Terrorists have tried to win control of Peru's government.

_____ **6.** Colombia earns money from exporting coffee and oil.

◆ Think and Apply

Categories   Read the words in each group. Decide how they are alike. Find the best title for each group from the words in dark print. Write the title on the line above each group.

Peru   Climates in the Andes   Colombia   Chile

1. _____

has borders on the Pacific Ocean and
   the Caribbean Sea
coffee is the main cash crop
has many drug traffickers

2. _____

Inca empire
largest Indian population
capital is on the Pacific coast

3. _____

hot land at sea level
cold land at 10,000 feet
frozen land at 15,000 feet

4. _____

about 2,000 miles long
cold climate in the south
about 100 miles wide

◆ Journal Writing

Write a paragraph that tells five facts about the Andean countries.

Using Latitude and Longitude

You learned that lines of **latitude** are east and west around Earth. Lines of **longitude** are north and south lines. Lines of latitude and longitude form a grid on maps and globes. These grids make it easy to find places.

The latitude of a place is written first, and the longitude is written next to it. Lima, Peru, is close to 12°S latitude. It is near 77°W longitude. We say that the latitude and longitude of Lima is 12°S, 77°W.

Look at the map below of the Andean countries. Circle the answer that completes each sentence.

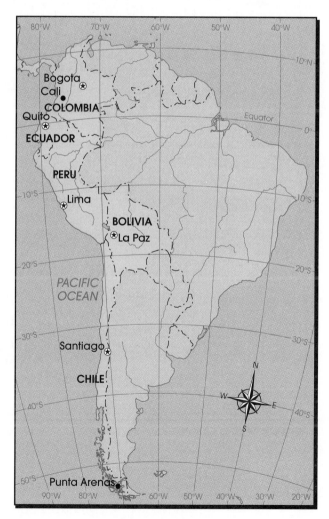

1. The latitude and longitude of Bogota, Colombia, is _____.

   60°N, 12°E   5°N, 74°W   80°S, 30°E

2. The city with the latitude and longitude of 0°, 78°W is _____.

   Quito   Bogota   Santiago

3. The city with the latitude and longitude of 16°S, 68°W is _____.

   Punta Arenas   La Paz   Quito

4. The latitude and longitude of Santiago, Chile, is _____.

   15°N, 105°E   75°N, 123°E

   33°S, 71°W

5. The city with the latitude and longitude of 53°S, 71°W is _____.

   Lima   Cali   Punta Arenas

CHAPTER 11

Understanding Latin America

Think About As You Read

1. Why are poverty and rapid population growth problems in Latin America?
2. How does the lack of transportation hurt Latin America?
3. What problems can a nation have with a one-crop economy?

New Words

- ◆ land reform
- ◆ rapid population growth
- ◆ illiteracy
- ◆ one-crop economy
- ◆ communism

People and Places

- ◆ Pan American Highway

Mr. Sanchez grows coffee on a large plantation in Colombia. There are hundreds of workers on his plantation. Mr. Sanchez is rich because he earns a lot of money by exporting his coffee. But his plantation workers are very poor. They earn low salaries. They struggle to have enough food for their families. The difference between the rich and the poor is one of many problems in Latin America. In this chapter you will learn about six problems in this region. You will find out how Latin Americans are working to solve these problems.

Poverty and Rapid Population Growth

The first problem is poverty. Millions of people in Latin America are very poor. Many farmers are poor because they do not own enough land to grow cash crops. Subsistence farmers struggle to grow enough to feed their families. Millions of people are poor because they do not have jobs. Other people have jobs that pay

About one third of the people in Latin America are under the age of 15 because of the region's rapid population growth.

very low salaries. Many people have moved to the United States to find jobs and earn more money.

Every day, poor people move to the large cities of Latin America. There they hope to find better jobs. They live in slums that surround the cities. The cities are growing fast. They are becoming crowded. The cities do not have enough schools, hospitals, and services for all the people in the slums.

Latin American governments are working to end poverty. Some governments are building places in the cities where poor families can live. Some governments are using **land reform**. Land reform happens when the government buys large plantations. Then they divide the land into smaller farms. These farms are given to poor farmers. Land reform helps farmers have their own land. However, farmers also need better tools and seeds in order to grow larger crops.

A second problem in Latin America is **rapid population growth**. Rapid population growth means the population grows a lot each year. For example, in 1985 Mexico had 80 million people. In 1996 there were 96 million people. Many people believe the population of Latin America will double in 20 years. Rapid population growth is a problem because there are not enough jobs, food, and homes for all the people.

Millions of people live in poverty in Latin America.

Many farmers in Latin America are poor. Children often have to work on their family's farm instead of going to school.

There are two reasons why the population is growing fast. One reason is that Latin Americans like big families. Farmers want to have children who will help with the farm work. A second reason is that there is better health care today. Fewer young babies die. People are healthier and live longer. In some places people are trying to have smaller families.

Illiteracy and Problems Using Resources

The third problem is **illiteracy**. Illiteracy means people do not know how to read and write. For example, in Guatemala almost half of the people cannot read. In El Salvador about one fourth of the people cannot read. People who cannot read cannot get good jobs.

Schoolchildren in Mexico

In many Latin American countries, young children go to school. But they are too poor to go to high school. Instead they work to help their families. In mountain villages and rain forest towns there are fewer schools and teachers. Children are not able to learn science, math, and computer skills. Without these skills, they will always work at low-paying jobs. To solve the education problem, many countries are building more new schools.

The fourth problem is the lack of good roads and transportation. Latin America is rich in resources. But many resources are in deserts and rain forests. Other resources are in mountains. There are not enough roads through deserts, rain forests, and mountains. So the people of the region cannot use many of their resources. To solve this problem, governments must build more roads and railroads.

To help trade, the countries of Latin America have built the Pan American Highway. The Highway includes about 30,000 miles of roads. These roads connect 17 countries in Latin America. But these roads are still not enough.

One Cash Crop Is Not Enough

The fifth problem is that too many countries depend on one cash crop to earn money. Colombia earns most of its money from exporting coffee. Most of the money Cuba earns is from sugarcane. Countries in Latin America sell some other cash crops, too. But most of their money comes from one main crop.

The Pan American Highway

Countries that earn most of their money from one crop have a **one-crop economy**. A one-crop economy can be a problem. What happens when there is little rain? What happens when the sugarcane crop or the coffee crop is not very large? What happens when the prices for these crops go down? Then these nations earn very little money.

To solve this problem, nations are planting different kinds of crops. Nations also need more factories and industries. They need to make many kinds of factory products that can be exported.

Many Latin American countries earn money from tourism. This helps the country change from a one-crop economy.

These elections in Nicaragua show that democracy is spreading in Latin America.

Changes in Latin America are making life better for the people living there.

The Need for Peace and Democracy

The sixth problem is civil wars and terrorism. You have learned how civil wars hurt Central America. In Chapter 10 you learned how terrorism has hurt Peru. In Mexico, Colombia, Peru, and some other countries, drug traffickers have their own soldiers. They attack and kill people who try to stop the illegal drug trade. In order for Latin America to become more developed, the region needs peace. All nations must work to stop terrorism. They need to end civil wars. The illegal drug trade must stop.

For many years people feared that Communists would win control of governments everywhere. Today **communism** has lost most of its power. Under communism the government controls a country's businesses. Today in Latin America only Cuba has a Communist government.

Democracy is spreading in Latin America. Countries such as Brazil, Peru, Chile, and Colombia were once ruled by dictators. They are now working to have democratic governments. People vote for their leaders in free elections. Most people are enjoying more freedom today.

Latin America has developed in many ways. Its people have better schools, better health care, and more jobs. With peace and better use of resources, Latin America will have more developed nations.

Chapter Main Ideas

1. Land reform is helping to end poverty in Latin America. Cities need better places for poor families to live.
2. The people of Latin America need to build better roads and transportation. Then they will be able to use the region's natural resources.
3. There are fewer dictators in Latin America today. Many nations are trying to be democracies.

◆ Vocabulary

Find the Meaning   Choose the word or words that best complete each sentence. Write your answers on the blank lines.

1. **Land reform** means breaking up _____ and giving land to poor farmers.

   ball fields   parks   plantations

2. Under **communism**, businesses are owned by the _____.

   rich people   government   students

3. **Illiteracy** means people do not know how to _____.

   paint   farm   read

4. If a country has **rapid population growth**, then it has more and more

   _____ each year.

   farms   people   cash crops

5. A country with a **one-crop economy** has one main _____.

   cash crop   subsistence crop   factory product

◆ Read and Remember

Finish the Paragraph   Use the words in dark print to finish the paragraph below. Write the words you choose on the correct blank lines.

high school   lower class   democratic   terrorists

Latin America has a very small upper class and a very large _____. So there are millions of poor people. Many poor children go to work instead of to _____. Many people have been killed by _____, civil wars, and drug traffickers. Now people in Latin America want peace. Many countries want to have _____ governments.

◆ Think and Apply

Find the Main Idea   Read the five sentences below. Choose the main idea and write it in the main idea box. Then find three sentences that support the main idea. Write them in the boxes of the main idea chart. There will be one sentence in the group that you will not use.

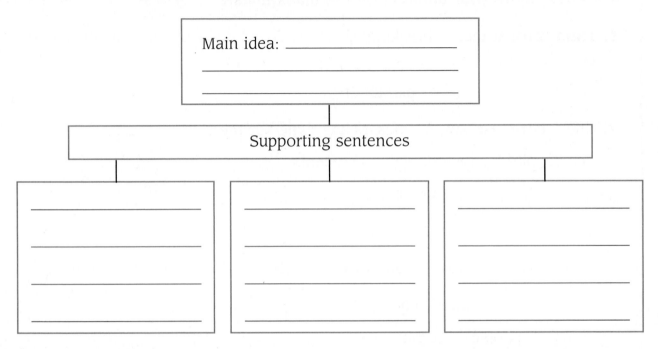

a. The population is growing too fast.

b. Latin America must solve many problems for its nations to become developed.

c. Better roads and railroads are needed.

d. Chile exports fruit to the United States.

e. Illiteracy is a problem in some nations.

◆ Journal Writing

Choose two problems that you think Latin America must solve. Write a paragraph that tells why nations must solve these problems.

UNIT 3

Western Europe

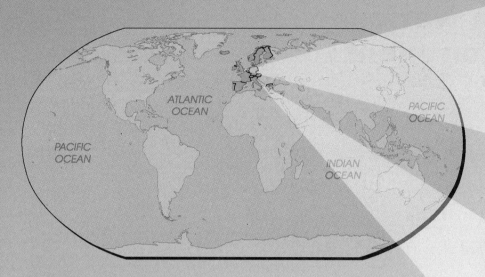

London, England

Venice, Italy

DID YOU KNOW?

▲ The first French fries were made in Belgium, not in France.

▲ Amsterdam, the capital of the Netherlands, was built on land that was once below the sea.

▲ There is no speed limit on some highways in Germany.

▲ The city of Venice, Italy, has about 400 bridges.

▲ Inside Italy is the world's smallest country, Vatican City. Inside this tiny country is the world's largest palace, the Vatican Palace. It has more than 1,000 rooms.

WRITE A TRAVELOGUE

For hundreds of years, the people of Western Europe spread their ideas and way of life to other parts of the world. Look through the photographs in this unit. What do you see in Western Europe that looks like where you live? Write a paragraph that describes what you see. Your travelogue should explain how the place is similar to where you live. After you read the unit, write two paragraphs that explain how two ideas have moved from Western Europe to other parts of the world.

THEME: MOVEMENT

95

CHAPTER 12

Western Europe: The Western Nations of a Small Continent

Where Can You Find?
Where can you find a small country with three official languages?

Think About As You Read

1. How have the seas helped Western Europe?
2. What types of government are found in Western Europe?
3. How are the countries in Western Europe different from each other? How are they alike?

New Words

◆ peninsula
◆ raw materials
◆ ocean currents
◆ fertile
◆ constitutional monarchy
◆ steel
◆ agriculture
◆ fertilizer

People and Places

◆ Western Europe
◆ Italy
◆ Germany
◆ North Sea
◆ Baltic Sea
◆ Mediterranean Sea
◆ North European Plain
◆ Alps
◆ Rhine River
◆ London
◆ Paris
◆ Christians
◆ Jews
◆ Muslims
◆ Switzerland

An American decided to buy a car made in Europe. Several countries in Western Europe make cars. Which country did the new car come from? It came from Italy. Cars are also made in Great Britain, Germany, France, and other countries in Western Europe. Cars are one of many products that are made in this region.

Geography and Climate of Western Europe

Europe is the second smallest continent. The region called Western Europe includes the countries shown on the map on page 97. Western Europe is only one third the size of the United States. But this region has many countries and more than 380 million people. It has far more people than the United States. This region has a high population density.

Western Europe is a large **peninsula**. A peninsula is land that has water on three sides. Many countries in

Map showing Western Europe with the following labels:

ICELAND, NORWAY, SWEDEN, FINLAND, ATLANTIC OCEAN, GREAT BRITAIN, IRELAND, North Sea, DENMARK, Baltic Sea, NORTH EUROPEAN PLAIN, London, GERMANY, Paris, Rhine R., FRANCE, SWITZERLAND, ITALY, SPAIN, PORTUGAL, Mediterranean Sea, GREECE, CYPRUS

MAP KEY
- ✱ Capital city
- –·– Border between countries
- ∿ River

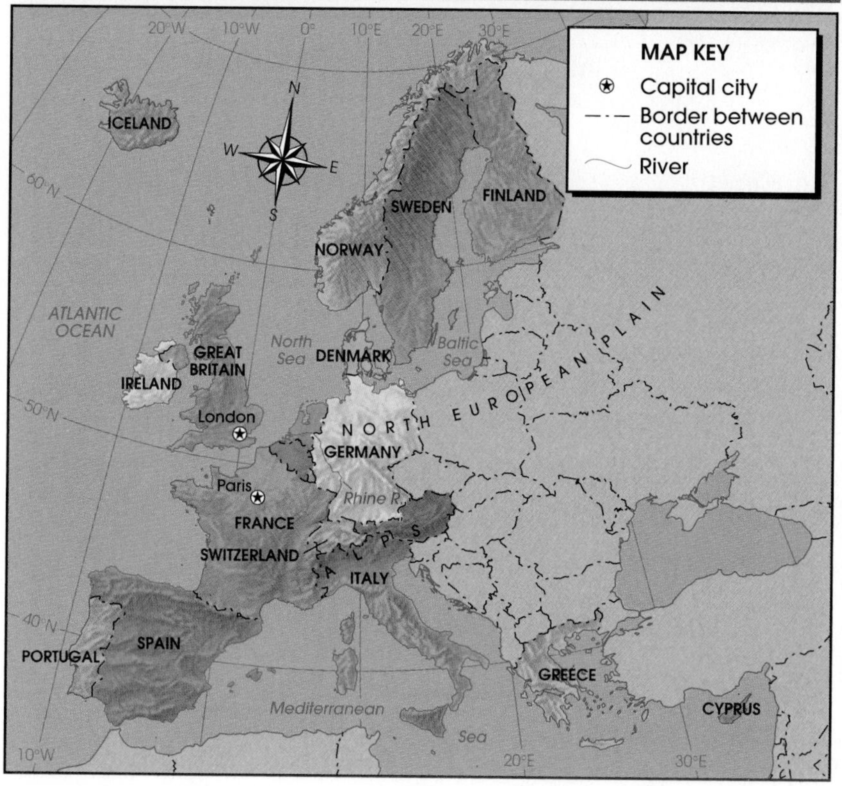

There are many countries in Western Europe. Which small country is located between France and Italy?

Western Europe are smaller peninsulas. Look at the map. Which countries in this region are peninsulas?

The seas are very important in Western Europe. No place in this region is more than 300 miles from a sea. The Atlantic Ocean is to the west. The Arctic Ocean, the North Sea, and the Baltic Sea are in the north. The Mediterranean Sea is to the south.

Europe has a long coast. It has many good ports. For hundreds of years, the seas have helped Europe. People from many countries in Europe have used the seas to sail to far-off lands. For hundreds of years, European countries ruled many colonies in Asia, Africa, and the Americas.

The seas have helped Europe in three other ways. First, people use the seas for fishing. Second, Europeans use the seas for shipping and trading. Trading ships carry goods and **raw materials** to Europe from many lands. Raw materials are natural resources that are used to make products. Countries in Western Europe make products from the raw materials. Then they sell the products to many nations.

A car factory in Italy

NORTH
ATLANTIC
DRIFT

CALIFORNIA
CURRENT

GULF
STREAM

ATLANTIC
OCEAN

PACIFIC
OCEAN

PACIFIC
OCEAN

INDIAN
OCEAN

PERU
CURRENT

MAP KEY
→ Cold water current
→ Warm water current

Warm water and cold water currents affect the weather around the world. Which two currents bring warm water in the direction of Western Europe?

Skiers in the Alps

Third, the seas help Western Europe by giving the region a mild climate. Did you know that Western Europe is as far north as Canada? But Western Europe has a much warmer climate. This happens because the warm **ocean currents** bring warmer air to most of Western Europe. Ocean currents are streams of water in the ocean. Ocean currents can be warm water or cold water. Warm ocean currents cross the Atlantic Ocean from the Americas to Western Europe. These warm ocean currents keep the region's climate mild.

Plains and mountains are the two main landforms in Western Europe. The North European Plain covers a large part of Western Europe. This large flat area stretches across the northern part of Europe. The soil on the plain is **fertile**. This land is very good for farming. Mountains cover the most northern parts of Europe. There are also mountain chains in parts of southern and central Europe. The Alps are Europe's most famous mountain chain. Many mountains in the Alps are covered with snow all year.

There are many different cultures in Western Europe. These dancers are from Italy.

Western Europe has many important rivers. This region also has many canals. The longest river in Western Europe is the Rhine River. The Rhine River is 820 miles long. It is much shorter than the Mississippi and Amazon rivers. The rivers and canals of Western Europe form important waterways. There are many port cities along these waterways. Ships carry goods from these ports to the seas. Then the goods are shipped to other countries.

Cities, People, Cultures, and Government

Most people in Western Europe live in cities. Most large cities in this region are located on rivers. Cities like London, England, and Paris, France, are famous.

Who are the people of Western Europe? Most Europeans are white. But many people from Africa and Asia have moved to Europe in order to find jobs.

Most people in Western Europe are Christians. They belong to Roman Catholic or Protestant churches. Jews and Muslims are smaller religious groups found in Western Europe.

There are many different countries in Western Europe. Each one has its own laws, stamps, and flags. Each country has its own culture with special foods, customs, and holidays. Almost every country has its own language. In some countries a few different languages are spoken. Switzerland is a small country

Each country in Western Europe has its own money.

The Rhine River

Train station in Western Europe

with three official languages. Most Europeans can speak two or more languages. Most children in Western Europe spend many years in school. Almost everyone knows how to read and write.

Most countries in this region are democracies. Some countries also have a king or a queen. The king or queen has little power. Instead a president or a prime minister leads the country. A democracy that has a king or a queen is a **constitutional monarchy**.

Natural Resources and Earning a Living

Western Europe is a region with developed nations. Most people have a high standard of living. The region has many factories and many industries.

Western Europe is not rich in natural resources. But it has some resources that are used in factories. Waterpower from rivers is used to make electricity. Many countries have coal and iron. Coal and iron are used to make **steel**. Some countries, such as Great Britain, have oil.

Many people in Europe work at service jobs. Others work at factory jobs. A small part of the population works at **agriculture**, or farming. Europeans use modern farm machines and lots of **fertilizer**. Fertilizers make soil more fertile to help grow more crops. Most countries grow enough food for their people. Some countries export food.

There is excellent public transportation throughout Western Europe. People can easily travel within their own country or from one country to another by train.

Four large countries in Western Europe are often in the news. These leading countries are Great Britain, France, Germany, and Italy. In the next chapters, you will learn why these countries are important.

Chapter Main Ideas

1. Western Europe is a large peninsula. Many countries in the region are smaller peninsulas.
2. Most of the countries of Western Europe are democracies. Some are constitutional monarchies.
3. There are many countries, cultures, and languages in Western Europe.

◆ Vocabulary

Finish Up   Choose the word or words in dark print that best complete each sentence. Write the word or words on the correct blank line.

steel   **fertilizer**   **ocean currents**   **peninsula**   **agriculture**

1. A _____ is land that has water on three sides.

2. Streams of water in the sea are called _____.

3. Coal and iron are used to make _____.

4. Another word for farming is _____.

5. To grow more crops, farmers improve the soil by adding _____.

◆ Read and Remember

Find the Answer   Put a check (✔) next to each sentence that tells why Western Europe is a region with developed nations. You should check five sentences.

_____ **1.** Farmers grow enough food for the region.

_____ **2.** Western Europe has many factories.

_____ **3.** Each country has its own laws, stamps, and flag.

_____ **4.** Almost everyone can read and write.

_____ **5.** People speak many different languages in Western Europe.

_____ **6.** Ships bring to Europe raw materials that people use to make factory products.

_____ **7.** European ships carry factory products to many countries of the world.

_____ **8.** Europe is the second smallest continent.

◆ Think and Apply

Drawing Conclusions   Read each pair of sentences. Then look in the box for the conclusion you might make. Write the letter of the conclusion on the blank.

1. People use the seas for fishing.
   People use the seas for trading and shipping.

   Conclusion: _____

2. Western Europe is warmer than Canada.
   Western Europe's winters are not too cold, and summers are not too hot.

   Conclusion: _____

3. There are port cities on many rivers.
   People travel on rivers through many parts of Western Europe.

   Conclusion: _____

4. Western Europe has coal and iron.
   Western Europe has waterpower and some oil.

   Conclusion: _____

5. Each country in Western Europe has its own leaders, government, and money.
   Each country has its own culture and flag.

   Conclusion: _____

Conclusions
   A. Rivers are important in Western Europe.
   B. Western Europe has some of the resources it needs for its factories.
   C. Warm ocean currents give Western Europe a mild climate.
   D. The countries of Western Europe have different cultures.
   E. The seas help Western Europe.

◆ Journal Writing

Write a paragraph that tells why many people in Western Europe have a high standard of living.

CHAPTER 13

The United Kingdom: An Island Country

Where Can You Find?
Where can you find Great Britain's oil?

Think About As You Read

1. What is the United Kingdom?
2. How have the seas helped the United Kingdom?
3. How did the Industrial Revolution change the United Kingdom?

New Words

- petroleum
- natural gas
- Act of Union
- Industrial Revolution
- revolution
- ethnic groups
- monarchs
- world power

People and Places

- United Kingdom
- Queen Elizabeth
- English Channel
- England
- Scotland
- Wales
- Northern Ireland
- Ireland
- Thames River
- Buckingham Palace
- British Empire
- Channel Tunnel
- Folkestone
- Calais

Canada and Jamaica have a queen, but she does not live in those countries. Her home is in the United Kingdom. Queen Elizabeth is the queen of Canada, Jamaica, the United Kingdom, and many other countries. In this chapter you will read about the United Kingdom, the home of Queen Elizabeth.

What Is the United Kingdom?

The United Kingdom is a country that is separated from the rest of Europe by the English Channel. The country has several islands. Great Britain is the largest island of the United Kingdom. Sometimes the entire country is called Great Britain. England, Scotland, and Wales are on the island of Great Britain. Northern Ireland is the fourth part of the United Kingdom. It is on the northern part of the island of Ireland. The United Kingdom's full name is the United Kingdom of Great Britain and Northern Ireland.

The people of the United Kingdom are often called the British. English is their official language. More than

The United Kingdom is an island country. What separates this country from the rest of Europe?

Flag of the United Kingdom

MAP KEY
- City
- ✪ Capital city
- –·– Border between countries
- ⌒ River

A lake in the mountains of Scotland

58 million people live in the United Kingdom. Most of these people live in England. England is the largest part of the United Kingdom.

Landforms, Seas, and Cities

The United Kingdom has a variety of landforms. Mountains cover large parts of Scotland and Wales. Hills cover much of Northern Ireland and northern England. Plains cover southern England. Southern England has the best farmland in the United Kingdom.

Seas surround the United Kingdom. The Atlantic Ocean is to the west. The North Sea is to the east. The English Channel is to the south. Seas are important to the United Kingdom. No place in this country is more than 75 miles from a sea. Warm ocean currents give the country a mild climate. The currents also bring much rain. The country has a long coast with many good harbors. So the British do a lot of shipping and trading. The British also catch and eat plenty of fish.

The Thames River is the country's busiest waterway. It is in southern England. Ships on the Thames River carry British goods to the English Channel. From there British ships sail to many countries.

Tourists in London enjoy a visit to Buckingham Palace.

Most British people live in cities. London, the country's capital, is the largest city. It is a busy port on the Thames River. Tourists enjoy visiting London's museums, stores, and theaters. In the summer they can visit the queen's home at Buckingham Palace.

Natural Resources and Earning a Living

The United Kingdom is not rich in natural resources. Its most important resource is oil. Oil is also called **petroleum**. Britain's oil is in the ground under the North Sea. Britain also has **natural gas** and coal. Natural gas is a type of fuel. Coal is mined in England and Wales. Great Britain has enough oil, natural gas, and coal for its own needs. It also exports some oil.

The British take oil from the ground under the North Sea.

Most British people work at service jobs. Many work in factories. Still others work at shipping and trading. Most people enjoy a high standard of living.

A small part of the population works at farming. Britain's main crops are wheat and other grains. Most British farmers also raise sheep. The British are good farmers. But their climate is not hot enough to grow such crops as bananas, oranges, and pineapples. So the British import about one third of their food.

The United Kingdom's History

Long ago, England, Wales, Scotland, and Ireland were independent countries. In 1707 a law was passed

Queen Elizabeth

called the **Act of Union**. With that law England, Wales, and Scotland became one nation.

In 1801 another Act of Union added Ireland to Great Britain. But many Catholics in Ireland did not want to be part of Great Britain. In 1921 the southern part of Ireland became a separate country. Northern Ireland remained part of the United Kingdom.

During the 1700s the **Industrial Revolution** began in England. This **revolution** was a change from making products by hand in homes to making products by using machines in factories. The United Kingdom became the world's first industrial nation. It used its coal and iron in its new factories. It used the seas to ship factory products to many countries.

During the 1700s the British began building a huge empire. By 1900 the British Empire had colonies in every part of the world. Great Britain got raw materials for its factories from these colonies. After 1945 most British colonies became free.

Today 50 countries that had been part of the British Empire are members of the British Commonwealth. Queen Elizabeth is the queen of the United Kingdom and 15 other Commonwealth countries.

Immigrants have moved to the United Kingdom from many Commonwealth countries. Today there are many **ethnic groups** in the United Kingdom. Many Africans and Asians in Great Britain do not live as well as other British people. The government is trying to find ways to help all people.

The Government of the United Kingdom

The United Kingdom is a constitutional monarchy. In a constitutional monarchy, the king or queen has very little power. Long ago, England's kings and queens, or **monarchs**, made all laws. Slowly, over hundreds of years, these monarchs lost their power. Parliament, the country's lawmakers, slowly grew more powerful. Today Parliament makes all laws. Queen Elizabeth does not make laws. She is a symbol of the nation. Most British people love their queen.

People of different ethnic groups from around the world live in the United Kingdom.

British soldiers have been in Northern Ireland for many years.

The British are proud of their government. It was the first democracy in Western Europe. The British vote for people to make laws for them in Parliament. The prime minister is the leader of Parliament and of the entire country.

Looking at the Future

In the late 1960s, fighting began between Catholics and Protestants in Northern Ireland. Many British soldiers were sent to Northern Ireland. The fighting in Northern Ireland has lasted more than thirty years. In 1994 the fighting stopped for a while. Will peace come to Northern Ireland? Will Northern Ireland remain part of the United Kingdom? No one knows these answers.

The United Kingdom no longer rules a huge empire. But the United Kingdom continues to be a **world power**. The British are proud that their small nation is an important leader among the countries of the world.

Parliament building in London

Chapter Main Ideas

1. England, Scotland, Wales, and Northern Ireland form the United Kingdom.
2. The United Kingdom used the seas to build a huge empire. Today it uses the seas for trade.
3. Great Britain became the world's first industrial nation. It got raw materials for its factories from colonies in the empire.

The Channel Tunnel

For hundreds of years, people dreamed of building a tunnel under the English Channel. That dream came true in 1994. After six years of work, the Channel Tunnel was finished! Trains began traveling through the tunnel between England and France. The Channel Tunnel, also called the Chunnel, was built at the most narrow part of the English Channel. The tunnel joins the city of Folkestone, England, with the city of Calais, France.

The Channel Tunnel is in the region of Western Europe. The region's technology and industry made it possible to build the tunnel. It cost $15 billion to build.

Today the Channel Tunnel makes it possible to travel between London and Paris in about three hours. The train ride through the Channel Tunnel takes only 20 minutes. Only trains can travel through the tunnel. But special trains can carry cars and trucks through the Channel Tunnel.

For hundreds of years, people needed ships to cross the English Channel. Today people can cross the English Channel by train through the Channel Tunnel.

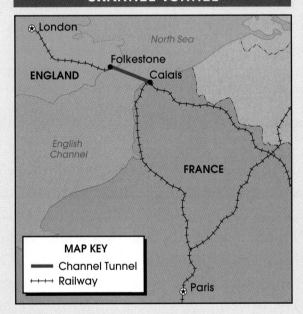

CHANNEL TUNNEL

London
North Sea
Folkestone
ENGLAND
Calais
English Channel
FRANCE

MAP KEY
—— Channel Tunnel
+++++ Railway

Paris

Write a sentence to answer each question.

1. Place   How is the Channel Tunnel different from every other place?

_____

2. Human/Environment Interaction   How has the Channel Tunnel changed the United Kingdom and France?

_____

3. Region   In what kind of region is the Channel Tunnel?

_____

◆ Vocabulary

Finish the Paragraph Use the words in dark print to finish the paragraph below. Write the words you choose on the correct blank lines.

monarch   **Act of Union**   **Industrial Revolution**   **petroleum**

England, Scotland, and Wales became one country in 1707 when a law called

the _____ was passed. During the 1700s England was the first

country to become a nation where products were made by machines in factories.

This change was called the _____. In England's democracy the

queen, or _____, has little power. The United Kingdom now gets

oil, or _____, from the North Sea.

◆ Read and Remember

Matching Each item in Group B tells about an item in Group A. Write the letter of each item in Group B next to the correct answer in Group A.

Group A

_____ **1.** Northern Ireland

_____ **2.** Parliament

_____ **3.** English Channel

_____ **4.** Commonwealth

_____ **5.** Great Britain

_____ **6.** London

Group B

A. This is the group that makes laws in the United Kingdom.

B. This is another name for the United Kingdom.

C. In this part of the United Kingdom, Catholics and Protestants have fought for many years.

D. This capital city is on the Thames River.

E. This is a group of nations that were part of the British Empire.

F. This body of water separates the United Kingdom from the continent of Europe.

Find the Main Idea Read the five sentences below. Choose the main idea and write it in the main idea box. Then find three sentences that support the main idea. Write them in the boxes of the main idea chart. There will be one sentence in the group that you will not use.

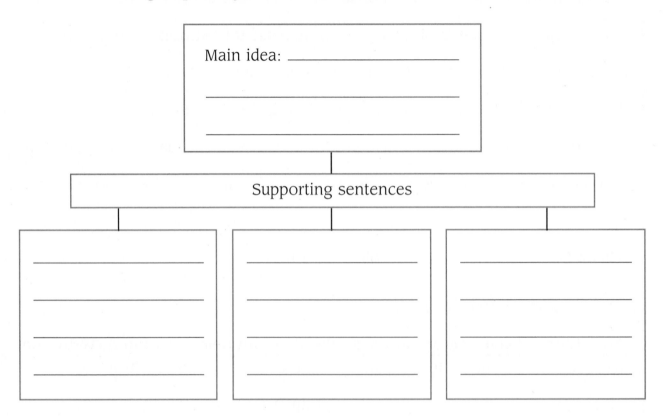

Main idea: _____

_____

_____

Supporting sentences

a. The British used the seas for trading.

b. Mountains cover large parts of Scotland and Wales.

c. The seas have helped Britain in many ways.

d. The British catch and eat a lot of fish.

e. The British used the seas to build an empire.

◆ **Journal Writing**

Journal Writing Imagine you are telling a friend to visit the United Kingdom. Write a paragraph with three or more reasons to visit the United Kingdom.

Reading a Bar Graph

Special drawings called **graphs** can help us compare facts. The graph below is called a **bar graph**. It shows facts by using bars of different lengths. This bar graph shows populations. By looking at the length of the bars, you can tell the population of each part of the United Kingdom. You can also compare the populations of the four different parts of the country.

Look at the bar graph below. Then circle the answer to each question.

1. What is the population of Northern Ireland?

15,000,000   1,640,000   7,500,000

2. What is the population of Wales?

2,900,000   12,300,000   35,200,000

3. What is the population of England?

48,700,000   30,420,000   6,400,000

4. What is the population of Scotland?

42,900,000   26,300,000   5,130,000

Write the answer to each question below.

1. Which country has the largest population?

_____

2. Which country has the smallest population?

_____

3. What conclusion can you draw about the population of the four parts of the United Kingdom?

_____

_____

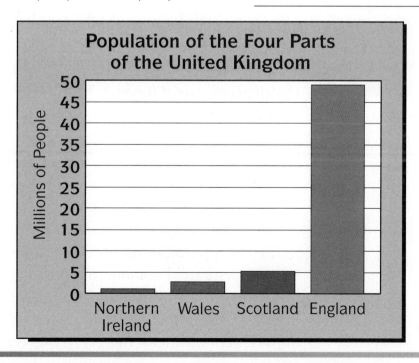

CHAPTER 14

France: A Leader of Farming and Industry

Think About As You Read

1. What kinds of landforms and climates are in France?
2. How do France's resources help its farms and factories?
3. What is special about France's culture?

New Words

◆ Mediterranean climate
◆ bullet trains
◆ uranium
◆ nuclear energy
◆ nuclear power plant
◆ manufacture
◆ cafés
◆ universities
◆ unemployment

People and Places

◆ Corsica
◆ Pyrenees Mountains
◆ Mont Blanc
◆ French Riviera
◆ Seine River
◆ Marseilles
◆ Eiffel Tower
◆ Algeria

Two American friends want to visit a country in Western Europe. One friend wants to be in northern Europe. She wants to see a big city with museums. The other friend wants to visit southern Europe. She wants to swim at a beach on the Mediterranean Sea. They can visit the same country if they visit France.

Landforms and Climate

France has the largest land area of any country in Western Europe. Find France on the map on page 113. The Atlantic Ocean is to the west. The English Channel is to the north. The Mediterranean Sea is to the south. The island of Corsica belongs to France. It is in the Mediterranean Sea.

Like the United Kingdom, the northern part of France has a mild climate. Southern France has a **Mediterranean climate**. This climate has long, hot, dry summers and short, rainy winters. Many nations on the Mediterranean Sea have this type of climate.

FRANCE

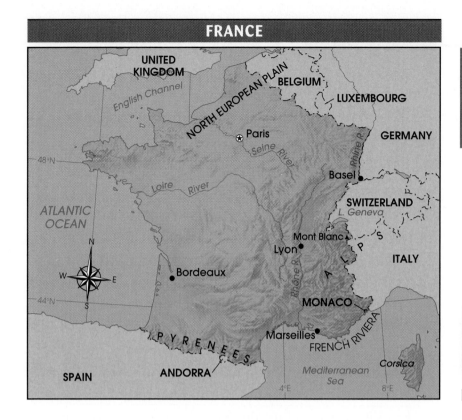

France has several different landforms, including plains and mountains. Which mountains are located between France and Spain?

France's flag

Plains cover more than half of France. The North European Plain covers northern France. Paris, the capital of France, is on this plain. This region has many farms and industries. Plateaus cover the northeastern part of the country.

In the southwest of France, the Pyrenees Mountains separate France from Spain. In the east the Alps Mountains separate France from Italy and Switzerland. One mountain in the Alps, Mont Blanc, is the tallest mountain in Western Europe.

The famous French Riviera is in the southeast. It has beautiful beaches on the Mediterranean Sea. Many tourists from around the world visit the Riviera.

Movement: Transportation in France

There are five important rivers in France. Paris was built on the Seine River. The Rhine River forms part of France's border with Germany. Canals join the rivers together. Ships can travel from the North Sea down the rivers and canals of France to the city of Marseilles. Marseilles is a city on the Mediterranean Sea. It is France's busiest port.

Mont Blanc

The waterways are just one type of transportation in France. Most families have their own cars. The country has excellent highways. Paris has subway trains. Railroad trains run throughout the country. France has some of the world's fastest trains. These **bullet trains** travel faster than 180 miles an hour. They go from Paris to other French cities. Some of these bullet trains go to other countries in Europe.

Bullet train

Natural Resources, Industries, Farms, and Cities

France is a rich country with many farms and many industries. Most people enjoy a high standard of living. But France was not always a rich country. When World War II ended in 1945, much of the country had been destroyed. The United States helped France rebuild its cities and factories.

France has some of the natural resources it needs to be an industrial country. It has coal and iron. It has bauxite for making aluminum. France also has a mineral called **uranium**. Uranium is used to make **nuclear energy**. France has little oil and natural gas. So the French make three fourths of their electricity in **nuclear power plants**.

France is an industrial leader. The French **manufacture**, or make, steel, planes, and weapons. They make fine perfumes and clothing. Computers,

France gets most of its electricity from nuclear power plants like this one in the Rhone River Valley.

Both tourists and people who live in Paris enjoy meals in the city's many sidewalk cafés.

chemicals, trains, and cars are some other French products. Only the United States, Japan, and Germany make more cars than France. French factory products are sold to many countries.

France also exports many foods. France has fertile soil for farming. Only a small part of the population works in agriculture. But the French grow more food than any other country in Western Europe. The French are famous for their cheese and wine. They make more than 300 different kinds of cheese. They grow many kinds of grapes. They use these grapes to make different types of wine.

The French and Their Culture

France has 58 million people. Three fourths of the French people live in cities. Paris is the largest city. About 9 million people live in and around the capital. Paris has many factories. Millions of tourists visit Paris. They eat in its outdoor **cafés**, or restaurants. They enjoy art museums and boat rides on the Seine River. One of the most famous places to see is the Eiffel Tower. From the top of the Eiffel Tower, tourists can view Paris and the Seine River.

France is a democracy. The people of France vote for leaders to make their laws in France's Parliament. Every seven years the people of France vote for their president.

The Eiffel Tower near the Seine River in Paris

The French Riviera

The French have a special culture. Many of the world's greatest artists and writers have been French. The French people love their French language. They try not to speak other languages.

Cooking is a type of art for the French. Meals have to taste good and look good. The French make special meals using different types of sauces. People enjoy eating crisp French bread and hot onion soup with their meals. Desserts are also special.

Enjoying life is another part of French culture. All workers get five weeks of vacation time during the summer. They use vacation time to go to the beach, to travel, and to go camping. They enjoy sitting in a café while watching people walk by on the sidewalk.

Education is important to the French. All children must go to school for ten years. Many students study in **universities** after they finish high school.

French desserts

Who are the people of France? Most French are white people. They come from families that have lived in Europe for a long time. Most people are Catholics. But there are also Muslims and Jews. About four million people are immigrants from southern Europe, northern Africa, and Asia. Many immigrants come from countries like Algeria that were once ruled by France. Most immigrants do not live as well as other French people. Many immigrants do not have jobs. **Unemployment** is a problem in France. More than ten percent of France's people do not have jobs.

The French are proud people. They love their language and their culture. They are proud of their many farms and factories. They are proud that France is a world power. France is a leader in Europe and in the world today.

Chapter Main Ideas

1. France is a leader of industry and farming in Western Europe. It has a high standard of living.
2. France has excellent transportation because of its highways, trains, and waterways.
3. The French are proud of their language and their special culture.

◆ Vocabulary

Analogies   Use the words in dark print that best complete the sentences.

Mediterranean   **manufacturing**   **unemployment**
uranium   **university**

1. Restaurant is to café as school is to _____.

2. Farming is to crops as _____ is to factory products.

3. Tropical climate is to Brazil as _____ climate is to Riviera.

4. Bauxite is to aluminum as _____ is to nuclear energy.

5. Not being able to read is to illiteracy as not having a job is to

_____.

◆ Read and Remember

Complete the Geography Organizer   Complete the geography organizer
below with information about France.

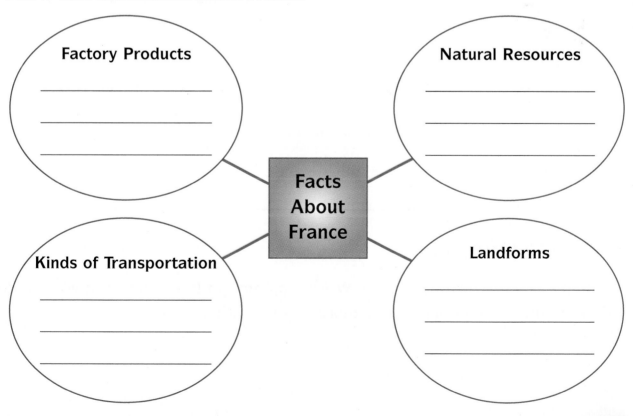

Factory Products

Natural Resources

Facts About France

Kinds of Transportation

Landforms

Write the Answer   Write one or more sentences to answer each question.

1. What type of weather is found in a Mediterranean climate?

_____

2. What is the busiest port in France?

_____

3. What types of trains are used in France?

_____

4. Where is nuclear energy made?

_____

◆ Think and Apply

Fact or Opinion   Write **F** next to each fact below. Write **O** next to each opinion. You should find three sentences that are opinions.

_____ **1.** There are mountains in the eastern part of France.

_____ **2.** France grows more food than any other nation in Western Europe.

_____ **3.** The French make many kinds of wine and cheese.

_____ **4.** The French Riviera has the best beaches in the world.

_____ **5.** The French manufacture cars, trains, planes, and clothing.

_____ **6.** Paris is the most beautiful city in the world.

_____ **7.** Many tourists visit the Eiffel Tower.

_____ **8.** France has too many immigrants.

◆ Journal Writing

Imagine you are visiting France. Write a paragraph that tells what you would do in France. Tell about four or more places you would visit.

Understanding Circle Graphs

A **circle graph** is a circle that has been divided into parts. Each part looks like a piece of pie. All the parts make up the whole circle. All the parts equal 100 **percent**.

The circle graph on this page shows how people earn a living in France. The three groups of workers make up the whole working population, or work force, in France.

Look at the circle graph. Then use the information on the graph to finish each sentence. Write the answers you choose on the correct blanks.

1. People who work in industry are

_____ percent of
the work force.

2. People who work in agriculture are

_____ percent of the
work force.

3. People who work at service jobs are

_____ percent of the
work force.

4. The largest group in the French work

force does _____.

5. The smallest group in the work force

does _____.

The Work Force in France

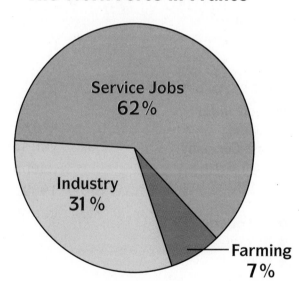

CHAPTER 15

Germany: One United Country

Think About As You Read

1. Why was Germany divided into two countries after World War II?
2. How did Germany become a united country again?
3. What problems does Germany have today?

New Words

- defeated
- national anthems
- Berlin Wall
- chancellor
- unification
- currency
- Holocaust

People and Places

- Adolf Hitler
- Poland
- East Germany
- West Germany
- Berlin
- East Berlin
- West Berlin
- Helmut Kohl
- Hamburg
- Munich
- Dachau
- Katarina Witt

Imagine what it would be like if you were not allowed to visit family or friends who lived nearby. How would you feel if it were not possible to call them on the telephone? This is what it was like in Germany before 1989. At that time Germany was divided into two countries. It had been divided soon after World War II ended. Today Germany is one country again. In this chapter you will learn why Germany was divided. You will learn how a united Germany is now an industrial leader.

Why Were There Two Germanys?

In 1933 Adolf Hitler became dictator of Germany. Hitler made all laws for the country. There was little freedom in Hitler's Germany. Hitler made Germany's army larger and stronger. In 1939 Germany attacked its neighbor, Poland. This was the start of World War II. Millions of soldiers from many nations fought in World War II. During the war large areas of Europe

GERMANY

Germany has several large rivers that are used for trade and transportation. Which two cities in Germany are located on rivers?

Germany's flag

were destroyed. Finally in 1945, Germany was **defeated**. The war ended.

The United States, Great Britain, France, and the Soviet Union had defeated Germany in 1945. After the war those four nations controlled different parts of Germany. The Soviet Union controlled the eastern part. It became East Germany. It had a Communist government. There was little freedom in East Germany. The rest of Germany became the country called West Germany. The people in both countries spoke German. But the two Germanys had their own laws, **national anthems**, flags, and money. Look at the map on this page of the two Germanys.

The United States helped rebuild West Germany after the war. It became a strong industrial country. It also became a democracy. People in West Germany had a much higher standard of living than the people of East Germany. They also enjoyed more freedom.

Berlin had been the capital of Germany before 1945. Berlin was in East Germany. After the war, Berlin was divided into two cities. East Berlin was a Communist city. It was East Germany's capital. West Berlin was a

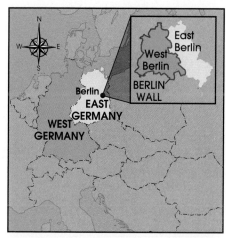

Divided Germany and divided Berlin

The Berlin Wall was torn down in 1989. Also at that time people were allowed to travel between East Germany and West Germany.

German Chancellor Helmut Kohl

free city inside East Germany. The people of West Berlin enjoyed freedom and a high standard of living.

Millions of East Germans wanted more freedom and a higher standard of living. So they ran away to West Berlin. From West Berlin they could go to West Germany. The Communist leaders decided to stop people from leaving East Berlin. In 1961, they built the **Berlin Wall**. The Berlin Wall separated East and West Berlin. It was 99 miles long. The Berlin Wall made it very hard for East Germans to escape to West Berlin.

For many years the Communists kept the East Germans and the West Germans apart. Families could not visit each other. Friends could not make telephone calls to each other. But Germans dreamed about a time when their country would be united again.

How Did Germany Become a United Country?

In 1989 the East Germans tore down the Berlin Wall. People in the two Berlins could visit each other again. Berlin became one city again. On October 3, 1990, East Germany and West Germany became one united nation. People throughout Germany danced with joy. October 3 is now celebrated as a holiday each year. This holiday is called the Day of German Unity.

In December 1990, all Germans voted in national elections. Helmut Kohl became the **chancellor**, or leader, of Germany. He had been West Germany's chancellor for many years.

Most Germans are happy about **unification**, or uniting into one country. But unification has been difficult. West Germany's money became the **currency**, or money, for all of Germany. So East German money had to be changed. Products in the united Germany cost more than products had cost in East Germany. The people of East Germany have found it hard to buy these more expensive products. Many East Germans lost their jobs and could not find work in the united country.

The people of West Germany have had to pay higher taxes in order to pay for unification. These taxes have paid for new roads, railroads, and factories in East Germany.

Even though unification has not been easy, Germans are very proud of their united country. They are happy that Berlin is a united city. In the year 2000, Berlin will be the nation's capital again.

Tourists at the Brandenburg Gate in Berlin

Germany's Landforms, Resources, and Economy

The North Sea and the Baltic Sea are north of Germany. Germany has ports on these seas. The seas are important for trading and fishing. The seas also give most parts of the country a mild climate.

The North European Plain covers northern Germany. The central part of the country has hills and low mountains. The south has many mountains. The tall Alps cover part of southern Germany.

Germany has many rivers. The Rhine River and its many canals are the country's busiest waterways.

Germany is famous for its beautiful countryside. These mountains are in southern Germany.

This worker is testing computer parts in a factory in Germany.

Education is important in Germany. This classroom is in a high school in what was once East Berlin.

Large ships on the Rhine carry oil, coal, iron, steel, and other products to different parts of Germany.

Germany is not rich in natural resources. But it has many forests. It has some coal and a lot of iron. Germany uses its coal to make about one third of its electricity. It imports large amounts of oil. It also imports many kinds of raw materials for its factories.

Today Germany is the industrial leader of Europe. There are factories in many parts of the country. German factories make steel, cars, and planes. They make machines, computers, tools, and many other products. Germans sell products to many countries.

Only a small part of Germany's population works at farming. The climate is too cool for farmers to grow enough food. Germany imports one third of its food.

Germany's People, Cities, and Future

Germany has more than 83 million people. It has more people than any other country in Western Europe. The Germans are hard workers who feel proud when they do good work. But they also try to enjoy life. They enjoy good food. They also like to sing and dance with friends. Education is important to Germans. All children spend at least nine years in school.

Most Germans live in cities. Most cities have excellent subways and other transportation. Germans are very proud of Berlin. It has the largest department store in all of Europe. Berlin also has a special museum about the Berlin Wall. Hamburg is a large northern port. Munich, in the south, has many theaters and museums.

Dachau is a city near Munich. Many Jews were killed there during World War II. During the war the Germans tried to kill all the Jews of Europe. The killing of Jews and other groups of people during the war is called the **Holocaust**. By the end of the war, six million Jews had been killed. Dachau has a museum that teaches about the Holocaust.

Germany is a rich country but it must solve some big problems. Many immigrants have moved to Germany. There are not enough jobs for them.

Unemployment is a problem in Germany today. The country does not have enough houses for all of its people. Pollution is another big problem. Factories have caused air pollution. River water has also become very dirty from all the factories. Germans are working to solve these problems. They want Germany to continue to be a great industrial country.

A highway in Germany

Chapter Main Ideas

1. Germany was divided into two countries after World War II. In 1990 unification made Germany one country again.
2. Germany is an industrial leader. But it must import food and raw materials.
3. Pollution and unemployment are problems in Germany today.

BIOGRAPHY

Katarina Witt (Born 1965)

Katarina Witt grew up in East Germany. She started ice-skating when she was five years old. The East Germans believed young Katarina could be an Olympic winner. So Communist leaders paid the country's best coach to train her. In 1984 Witt skated in the Olympic Games. She won a gold medal for East Germany. Four years later she won a second gold medal at the Olympics. The Communists rewarded her with cars and apartments.

Witt made many Germans angry when she spoke out against unification. Yet her life changed after unification. Witt could now decide for herself when or where she would skate. She was able to earn much more money. In 1992 Witt skated in the Olympics again. She skated for a united Germany, but she did not win a medal. Witt continues to skate in ice shows in Germany, the United States, and in other countries.

Journal Writing
Write a paragraph in your journal about Katarina Witt. Tell how Katarina's life changed after the unification of Germany.

◆ Vocabulary

Find the Meaning   Write the word or words that best complete each sentence on the blank lines.

1. When Germany was defeated in 1945, Germany had _____.

    won the war   lost the war   built new cities

2. A national anthem is a _____ for your country.

    song of praise   special food   dance

3. The unification of Germany means the country became _____.

    divided   more developed   united

4. The chancellor is the _____ of Germany.

    money   national anthem   leader

5. Currency is the _____ used by a country.

    language   money   culture

◆ Read and Remember

Write the Answer   Write one or more sentences to answer each question.

1. How was Germany divided after World War II?

    _____

2. How was the city of Berlin divided?

    _____

3. Why did many East Germans want to go to West Berlin?

    _____

4. Why did Communists in East Germany build the Berlin Wall?

    _____

5. When did Germany become a united country again?

_____

6. Why was unification hard for the German people?

_____

7. What is the main landform in southern Germany?

_____

8. What are some products that are made in German factories?

_____

9. What must Germany import?

_____

10. What are two problems in Germany today?

_____

◆ Think and Apply

Sequencing Write the numbers **1**, **2**, **3**, **4**, and **5** next to these sentences to show the correct order.

_____ Germans voted for Helmut Kohl to lead a united Germany.

_____ Germany attacked Poland and World War II began.

_____ The Berlin Wall was torn down.

_____ After Germany was defeated in World War II, the Soviet Union started a Communist government in East Germany.

_____ Communists built the Berlin Wall in 1961.

◆ Journal Writing

Imagine that you were a German who lived in East Berlin in 1989. Write a paragraph that tells what you would have done after the Berlin Wall was torn down.

Reading a Political Map

A **political map** helps you learn about countries. The map key on a political map uses symbols to show borders, cities, rivers, and other places.

Study the political map and its map key. Then answer each question.

1. What three countries are to the east of Germany?

_____

_____

_____

2. What seas are north of Germany?

_____

_____

3. What city in Germany is in the east?

_____

4. What city in Germany is in the south?

_____

5. What two countries are to the south of Germany?

_____

_____

6. What city is in northern Germany?

_____

7. What countries are west of Germany?

_____

_____

_____

_____

8. Name three rivers in Germany.

_____

_____

_____

Italy and Mediterranean Europe

Think About As You Read

1. How are the four countries in the Mediterranean region alike?
2. How are the three regions of Italy different from each other?
3. Why is Vatican City important?

New Words

- mountainous
- favorable balance of trade
- arches
- ruins
- monuments
- pope

People and Places

- Greece
- Sicily
- Sardinia
- Apennine Mountains
- Po River
- Po Valley
- Rome
- Tiber River
- Colosseum
- Vatican City
- Bologna
- Florence
- Venice

Italy is one of the oldest countries in Europe, but it is also one of the newest. It is old because it began more than 2,000 years ago. Italy is new because it did not become a united country until 1870. Today Italy is one of several European countries on the Mediterranean Sea.

The Mediterranean Region

Italy, Spain, Portugal, and Greece are four West European nations in the Mediterranean region. Mountains separate them from the rest of Europe. About one third of Western Europe's people live in this region. Italy has the largest population in this region. Italy has more than 57 million people.

The four Mediterranean countries are alike in some ways. They all have a Mediterranean climate. So their winters are rainy and their summers are long, hot, and dry. Mountains and hills cover much of the land. They have few rivers that can be used for transportation. These countries have few natural resources.

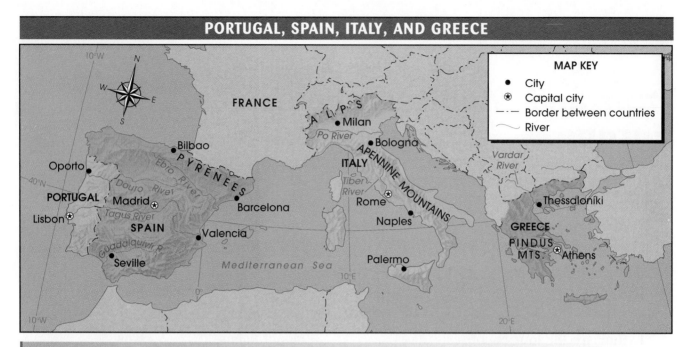

PORTUGAL, SPAIN, ITALY, AND GREECE

The four countries on this map have many things in common. They have a Mediterranean climate, mountainous land, and few natural resources. Which of these four countries does not have a coast on the Mediterranean Sea?

Olive trees

More people work at farming in the Mediterranean region than in the northern parts of Western Europe. Olive trees grow throughout this region. These countries export olives and olive oil. Except for Italy, this region has less industry than the rest of Western Europe. Spain, Portugal, and Greece have lower standards of living than the rest of Western Europe.

Religion is important to the people in this region. Most of the people in Spain, Portugal, and Italy are Roman Catholic. Most Greeks belong to the Greek Orthodox Church.

Italy: A Mediterranean Country

Italy is a long peninsula in the Mediterranean Sea. The country is shaped like a boot. The islands of Sicily and Sardinia in the Mediterranean Sea belong to Italy.

Most of Italy is **mountainous**. The Alps separate Italy from France and Switzerland. The Apennine Mountains cover a large part of the country from north to south. Some Apennines Mountains are volcanoes.

There are three regions in Italy. The northern region is the country's industrial region. Factories in the northern region make cars, steel, machines, shoes, and many other products. Some of the world's best sports cars are made in this region. Waterpower in this region is used to make about one fourth of Italy's electricity. The Po River is in northern Italy. Plains around the river form the Po Valley. The Po Valley has Italy's best farmland. Northern Italy is the country's richest region.

The second region is central Italy. This region surrounds the city of Rome. Rome is Italy's capital and its largest city. Plains and low hills near the western coast have good farmland.

Southern Italy is the third region. It is the poorest part of Italy. It is mountainous. The soil is not good for farming. So it is difficult to grow food in this region. People raise sheep and goats. Some people produce olive oil from olive trees. This region has few factories. Many people have moved from southern Italy to the north to get factory jobs. In the early 1900s, many people from southern Italy moved to the United States.

Today about ten percent of Italy's people earn a living by farming. These farmers grow most of the food Italy needs. Farmers grow large amounts of grapes for wine. Italy makes more wine than any other country.

About one third of the population works at factory jobs. More than half of the people earn a living at

Italy

Italy's flag

Northern Italy has some of the country's best farmland. The Alps are also found in this part of Italy.

Rome is a mixture of the very old and the very new. The ruins of the Colosseum are next to modern apartment buildings.

The Colosseum

service jobs. Many of these people work in the tourism industry. Italy earns billions of dollars each year from tourism.

Italy earns a lot of money from trade. Some of the products Italy exports are cars, shoes, cheese, wine, and olive oil. Italy has a **favorable balance of trade**. This means it exports more than it imports.

Italy's History and Government

About 2,500 years ago, people began to build the city of Rome. The city was built on seven hills near the Tiber River. The Romans then conquered much land and many people to create a huge empire. The Romans were great builders. They built many temples, theaters, roads, and **arches** in Rome and throughout their empire. The Romans ruled their empire for 900 years. In the year 476, the Roman Empire fell apart.

After the Roman Empire fell apart, Italy was made of many small states. Each state had its own laws and its own ruler. In the 1800s people began working to unite all the states. In 1870 Italy became one nation.

Today Italy is a democracy. A prime minister leads the country. People vote for members of Parliament.

Rome, Vatican City, and Other Cities in Italy

Two thirds of Italy's people live in cities. Rome has about 3 million people. It has fewer factories than other large cities in Europe. Most Romans work at government and service jobs. Others work in hotels and restaurants for tourists.

Rome is both a modern city and a very old one. The city has modern buildings, lots of cars, and a subway system. But in Rome you can also see **ruins**, or very old buildings, from the time of the Roman Empire. There are very old temples, fountains, statues, and **monuments**. You can see the Colosseum that the Romans built long ago. This huge theater had enough seats for 50,000 people. Today visitors can drive around the Colosseum on a modern six-lane highway.

Ancient Romans built arches to honor their leaders.

Inside the city of Rome is a tiny independent country. That country is Vatican City. It is also called the Vatican. It has its own flag, laws, money, and stamps. Less than 1,000 people live in this tiny country. But it is important because it has the government for the Roman Catholic Church. There are almost 1 billion people who belong to the Roman Catholic Church today. The **pope**, the world leader of the Catholic Church, is the ruler of the Vatican. Millions of people visit the Vatican each year.

Italy has other important cities. Bologna has Europe's oldest university. Florence, in central Italy, is famous for its paintings and statues. The city of Venice is in northern Italy. Venice was built on about 120 islands. People travel through the many canals of Venice on boats. The people of Italy are proud of their cities, their long history, and their modern industries.

Pope John Paul II in Vatican City

Chapter Main Ideas

1. Italy, Spain, Portugal, and Greece are the four Mediterranean countries of Western Europe. Italy has the most people and the highest standard of living.
2. Italy's history began in Rome 2,500 years ago.
3. Northern Italy is a rich industrial region. Southern Italy is a poorer region where people work at agriculture.

◆ Vocabulary

Match Up   Finish the sentences in Group A with words from Group B. Write the letter of each correct answer on the blank line.

Group A

Group B

1. A country that has many mountains is _____.

A. favorable balance of trade

2. Italy exports more goods than it imports, so it has a _____.

B. ruins

C. mountainous

3. The leader of the Roman Catholic Church is the _____.

D. monument

4. A building that was built to remember an event is a _____.

E. pope

5. In Rome you can see very old buildings, or _____, from long ago.

◆ Read and Remember

Where Am I?   Read each sentence. Then look at the words in dark print for the name of the place for each sentence. Write the name of the correct place on the blank after each sentence.

Rome   Vatican City   Greece   Bologna   Venice

1. "I am in a country where most people follow the Greek Orthodox religion."

   _____

2. "I am in a city in northern Italy where people travel on boats through canals."

   _____

3. "I am in Italy's capital and largest city." _____

4. "I am in an Italian city with the oldest university in Europe." _____

5. "I am in a tiny independent country inside the city of Rome." _____

Finish Up Choose the word or words in dark print that best complete each sentence. Write the word or words on the correct blank line.

Tiber River   Colosseum   industry   Apennines   Sardinia

1. The Alps and the _____ are two mountain chains in Italy.

2. Northern Italy has more _____ than southern Italy.

3. The islands of Sicily and _____ belong to Italy.

4. The city of Rome is on the _____.

5. Long ago the Romans built a huge theater called the _____.

◆ Think and Apply

Compare and Contrast Read each phrase below. Decide whether it tells about northern or southern Italy. If it tells about either region, write the number of the phrase in the correct part of the Venn diagram. If the phrase tells about all of Italy, write its number in the center of the diagram.

1. industrial region
2. Mediterranean climate
3. most people work at agriculture
4. richest region
5. poorest region

6. about 57 million people
7. most people are Roman Catholics
8. poor soil for farming
9. fertile Po Valley

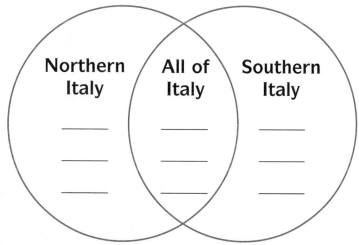

Northern Italy   All of Italy   Southern Italy

◆ Journal Writing

Write a paragraph in your journal that tells about the countries of the Mediterranean region. Tell one fact about each country in the region.

Reading a Physical Map

Italy and most other countries have several different landforms. Some places have low plains. Other areas have tall mountains. A **physical map** shows how high the land is in different places. From a physical map you can learn where there are low plains, hills, and high mountains. An **elevation key** is part of a physical map. The key uses different colors to show different elevations.

Circle the answer to each question.

1. What is the elevation of the Alps near France?

0–650 feet   650–1,500 feet   6,500–13,000 feet

2. What is the elevation of Mt. Etna?

less than 6,500 feet   10,902 feet   more than 13,000 feet

3. What is the highest elevation of the Apennine Mountains?

0–650 feet   650–1,500 feet   more than 1,500 feet

4. What is the elevation of Venice?

less than 650 feet

more than 1,500 feet

more than 6,500 feet

5. What is the elevation of Rome?

0–650 feet

650–1,500 feet

more than 13,000 feet

6. What can we conclude about the elevation of Italy's cities?

their elevation is high

their elevation is low

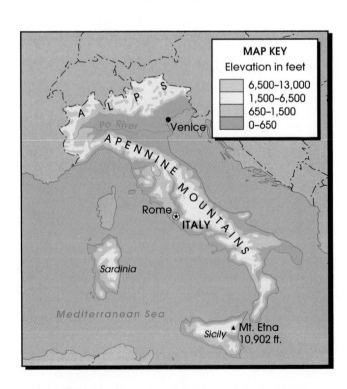

MAP KEY
Elevation in feet
6,500–13,000
1,500–6,500
650–1,500
0–650

CHAPTER 17

Understanding Western Europe

Where Can You Find?
Where can you find the leaders of a united Western Europe?

Think About As You Read

1. How has NATO helped Western Europe?
2. How are the countries of Western Europe solving energy and pollution problems?
3. How is the European Union helping Western Europe become more united?

New Words

◆ passport
◆ NATO
◆ Partnership for Peace
◆ hydroelectric power
◆ solar energy
◆ geothermal energy
◆ recycle
◆ European Community
◆ European Union
◆ euro

People and Places

◆ Turkey
◆ Norway
◆ Belgium
◆ Sweden
◆ Iceland
◆ Brussels

Imagine taking a train ride through several countries in Western Europe. At most borders, guards would not check your **passport**. Traveling from country to country in Western Europe is now almost as easy as traveling through different states of the United States. In the past it was not so easy. Today the countries of Western Europe are working together in new ways.

Western Europe Today and the Need for NATO

Today there is peace in Western Europe. But for hundreds of years, there were wars in this region. Europeans fought wars to rule their continent. They also fought wars to control colonies in Africa, Asia, and the Americas. In the 1900s most countries in Europe fought in World War I and World War II.

After World War II, the countries of Western Europe were afraid that the Soviet Union and other Communist countries would attack them. So they formed an organization called **NATO** to protect

MAP KEY
- NATO member
- Partnership for Peace member

ICELAND

SWEDEN

NORWAY

RUSSIA

UNITED KINGDOM

DENMARK

NETH.

POLAND

BELG.

GERMANY

UKRAINE

KAZAKSTAN

LUX.

FRANCE

SWITZ.

ITALY

PORTUGAL

SPAIN

GREECE

TURKEY

There are 16 countries in NATO. The United States and Canada are two members of NATO not shown on this map. Partnership for Peace (PfP) countries have joined with NATO to bring peace to countries that have wars. What are the names of two PfP nations?

NATO's flag

Air force planes from Turkey and the United States fly together for NATO.

themselves. NATO stands for the North Atlantic Treaty Organization. Thirteen Western European nations belong to NATO. Canada, Turkey, and the United States are also members. Soldiers from NATO nations will fight together if an enemy attacks a member.

Today communism is no longer a problem for Western Europe. So NATO's new goal is to bring peace to countries that have wars. Many countries in Eastern Europe are now working with NATO. They are not NATO members. They are part of a program called the **Partnership for Peace**, or PfP. Soldiers from PfP countries work with NATO soldiers. Some countries such as Poland and Hungary may soon be allowed to join NATO. Russia will be allowed to work more closely with NATO in the future.

Energy and Pollution Problems

Western Europe is an important industrial region. But many of the natural resources in this region have been used up. Today most countries in Europe import large amounts of raw materials from far-off nations.

Western Europe needs lots of energy for its cars, homes, and factories. Norway and the United Kingdom get oil from the North Sea. But many other countries must import oil. Many European countries do not want to import oil from other places because it is expensive. So they are trying to find other ways to make energy. Today France, Belgium, Switzerland, and other countries are using nuclear energy to make electricity. Italy, Sweden, Switzerland, and some other countries are using **hydroelectric power**, or electricity made from waterpower. Some countries like Greece are using energy from the sun, or **solar energy**. A few countries like Iceland have **geothermal energy**, or energy from hot places inside the earth.

Pollution is a very big problem in Western Europe. Cars and factories are causing air pollution. Air pollution becomes part of rain and snow and causes acid rain. Acid rain is destroying forests, fish, and lakes in many European countries.

Today Western Europe is trying to end pollution. Many countries have passed clean air laws. Cars and factories must be built so they send less pollution into the air. Some nations have passed clean water laws. The United Kingdom was one of those nations. The British worked hard to make the dirty Thames River clean again. Some beaches on the Mediterranean Sea have also been made clean and safe.

Europeans are working to protect their environment. Most people **recycle** old cans, bottles, paper, and plastic. Factories are using less paper, cardboard, and

Europeans want to end pollution.

This place in southern Iceland uses geothermal energy to make electricity.

The European Union

Europe's new currency, the euro

plastic to wrap products such as candy, toothpaste, and televisions. By using less wrapping materials, there will be less trash to harm the environment.

Working for a United Europe

Some people hope that one day all the countries of Europe will unite and become one country. In 1957 six countries of Western Europe began working together as the **European Community**. Members of the European Community worked to have more trade with each other. More nations later joined the European Community. In 1994 the European Community became the **European Union**. It is also called the EU. Fifteen Western European countries are part of the EU. The leaders of the EU meet in Brussels, Belgium.

The European Union is working for a united Europe. People no longer need passports to cross the border from one member nation to another. People from one EU nation can live or work in any other EU country.

The European Union helps trade between its members. There are no tariffs on goods that are bought or sold between EU members. The European Union now exports more goods than the United States.

Today every country in Western Europe has its own money. In 1999 all EU members will use the same currency. The new currency will be called the **euro**.

The people in Western Europe are proud of their countries. They are proud of their cultures. But they are also proud to be Europeans. Can the EU join all the countries together to form one country? Many people are working toward this goal. Perhaps one day there will be a United States of Europe.

Chapter Main Ideas

1. Western Europe is a developed region. It depends on imported raw materials for its factories.
2. Many countries are working to solve the problems of air pollution, acid rain, and water pollution.
3. The countries of Western Europe are working together through NATO and the European Union.

USING WHAT YOU'VE LEARNED

◆ Vocabulary

Forming Word Groups Read each heading on the chart below. Then read each word in the vocabulary list on the left. Form groups of words by writing each vocabulary word under the correct heading.

Vocabulary List

NATO
hydroelectric
euro
solar
Partnership for Peace
European Community
geothermal
European Union
nuclear

Europeans Working Together	Types of Energy
1. ______	1. ______
2. ______	2. ______
3. ______	3. ______
4. ______	4. ______
5. ______	

◆ Read and Remember

Complete the Chart Use facts from the chapter to complete the chart. You can read the chapter again to find facts you do not remember.

Problems in Western Europe

	Europe Needs Raw Materials	Europe Needs a Lot of Energy	Pollution and Acid Rain
What is the problem?			
How are people solving the problem?			

Write the Answer   Write one or more sentences to answer each question.

1. Why was the North Atlantic Treaty Organization, NATO, formed?

_____

2. What is NATO's new goal?

_____

3. How are former Communist nations working with NATO?

_____

4. How does the European Union help trade between its members?

_____

◆ Think and Apply

Finding Relevant Information   Imagine you are telling your friend how the nations of Western Europe are working for a united Europe. Read each sentence below. Decide which sentences are relevant to what you will say. Put a check (✔) in front of the relevant sentences. You should find three relevant sentences.

_____ **1.** In 1957 six nations in Western Europe began working together for better trade.

_____ **2.** People who live in a European Union nation can live or work in any other European Union country.

_____ **3.** Today communism is no longer a problem for the countries of Western Europe.

_____ **4.** In 1999 all European Union countries will have the same currency.

_____ **5.** The British passed clean water laws to end pollution in the Thames River.

◆ Journal Writing

Journal Writing   Write a paragraph about two problems in Western Europe today. Tell how people are working to solve those problems.

UNIT 4

Eastern Europe and Russia and Its Neighbors

Budapest, Hungary

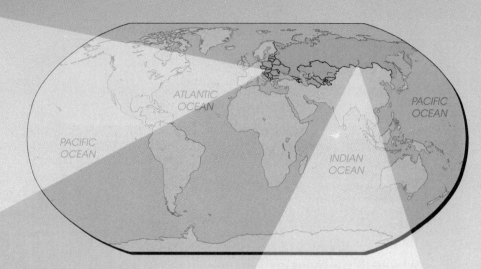

Lake Baikal, Russia

DID YOU KNOW?

▲ The world's longest train ride is 6,000 miles on Russia's Trans-Siberian Railroad.

▲ Moscow has the world's busiest subway system. It is used about 4 billion times each year.

▲ Lake Baikal in Russia is the world's deepest lake. More than 350 rivers flow into the lake, but only one flows out.

▲ Budapest, Hungary, is really two cities. They are Buda and Pest. They are on different sides of the Danube River.

WRITE A TRAVELOGUE

Imagine you are going to travel by train through Eastern Europe and Russia and its neighboring countries. Keep a travelogue about your trip. Which countries would you want to visit? Before reading Unit 4, write a paragraph about why you might want to visit those countries. After reading the unit, write two paragraphs about the ways that people and goods can move through this region.

THEME: MOVEMENT

A Changing Region

Think About As You Read

1. How did Communists win control of this region?
2. Why is this a changing region?
3. What are the landforms, climates, and resources of this region?

New Words

- **Commonwealth of Independent States**
- **czars**
- **Russian Revolution**
- **command economy**
- **free market economy**
- **continental climate**

People and Places

- **Russia**
- **Estonia**
- **Latvia**
- **Lithuania**
- **Ural Mountains**
- **Danube River**
- **Black Sea**

Eastern Europe and Russia and its neighboring countries form the region that is east of Western Europe. It is a region that is changing in the way people live, work, and choose government leaders.

A Huge Region

Eastern Europe and Russia and its neighbors form a huge region with land on two continents. The region covers the eastern part of Europe and the northern part of Asia. This region can be divided into three groups of countries. The first group is the countries of Eastern Europe. The second group includes three countries along the Baltic Sea—Estonia, Latvia, and Lithuania. These Baltic countries are in northern Europe. Russia and 11 smaller countries are the third part of the region. These 12 countries have formed a group called the **Commonwealth of Independent States**, or C.I.S.

This region contains many countries in both Europe and Asia. What mountain chain divides the western part of Russia from Siberia?

For more than forty years, Communists controlled the entire region. Today these countries do not have Communist governments. How did this happen?

The History of the Region

For hundreds of years, Russia was a country that was ruled by kings. The kings were called **czars**. They made all laws. Most Russians were very poor. The people did not have enough food. The czars did little to help the poor. By 1917 many Russians were angry. They wanted a different government. So in that year, angry Russians started a war called the **Russian Revolution**. During this fight Communists won control of Russia.

The Russians later took control of their neighboring countries. They formed one country called the Soviet Union. A Communist government ruled the entire Soviet Union. During World War II, the Soviet Union

A Russian czar and his family

The Russian people celebrated the end of communism in their country in 1991.

The three Baltic nations are the only part of the former Soviet Union that did not join the C.I.S.

MAP KEY
■ C.I.S.
— Former Soviet Union

took control of the three Baltic countries. They were forced to become part of the Soviet Union.

After the war, the Soviet Union forced the nations of Eastern Europe to have Communist governments. These countries were not part of the Soviet Union. But the Soviet Union controlled their governments.

There was little freedom in Eastern Europe and the Soviet Union. The Communists did not allow free elections. People could not speak out against their government. People could not travel to other countries. Freedom of religion was not allowed. People were afraid to practice their religions.

In these Communist countries, the government owned all farms, factories, and businesses. The government decided what crops farmers should grow. The government told factories what to make and what prices to charge. The government decided how much the workers should be paid. This type of controlled economy is called a **command economy**.

By 1989 many people wanted to change their Communist governments. Communism first ended in Poland. Then the Berlin Wall opened in East Germany. Other countries in Eastern Europe formed new governments that were not controlled by Communists. At the end of 1991, communism ended in the Soviet Union. The huge country fell apart. Russia became an independent country again. The other 14 countries that had been part of the Soviet Union also became free. Eleven of them formed the C.I.S. with Russia. The three Baltic countries did not join the C.I.S. Many countries in the region are trying to have democratic governments.

How Are Countries in the Region Alike and Different?

The countries of this region are different from each other. They have their own governments and their own languages. But they are also alike in some ways. All of these countries are less developed than the nations of Western Europe. People in Eastern Europe have a lower standard of living than the people in Western Europe. Most of the people living in the C.I.S. have an even lower standard of living. Eastern Europe has more industry and better farming than the C.I.S. But in many places throughout this region, people still use animals, not machines, to do farm work.

A free market economy helps businesses such as this shipyard in Poland.

The countries in this region are alike in another way. Today Communists no longer control the region. Most of the countries are changing to a **free market economy**. In a free market economy, people own and control companies, factories, farms, and businesses. The government does not own or control them. The United States, Canada, and Western Europe have free market economies. Many countries in the region are finding it difficult to change to a free market economy. Many products have become more expensive. Many people do not have jobs.

Landforms, Climates, and Resources

The North European Plain covers the northern part of this region. There is a lot of good farmland on the plains of Europe. The region also has mountains. The low Ural Mountains separate Europe from Asia. Most mountains are in the southern part of the region. Look at the map on page 145. Which areas are covered with plains? Which areas have mountains?

The Danube River

The Danube River is the most important river in this region. The Danube is 1,776 miles long. It flows south from Germany through many countries in Eastern

Parts of Eastern Europe are mountainous. People enjoy visiting the mountains during the winter to go skiing.

People in this region can speak out against their leaders now that communism has ended.

Europe. Then it runs into the Black Sea. The Danube is used for trade and transportation. There are many ports on this river. Like the Rhine River, water pollution is a big problem on the Danube.

Most of this region has a cold climate. Warm ocean currents from the Atlantic Ocean do not warm the region because the ocean is too far away. Many places have a **continental climate**. This means winters are long and very cold. Summers are short and hot. As you move north and east, the climate gets much colder. This region also gets less rain than Western Europe. In the southern part of the region, the climate is warmer. Some southern areas have a Mediterranean climate.

Parts of this region are rich in natural resources. Poland and some other Eastern European countries have coal. Russia has coal, oil, diamonds, and many other resources.

The end of communism has changed the way people live and work in Eastern Europe and Russia and its neighbors.

Chapter Main Ideas

1. Eastern Europe and Russia and its neighbors cover parts of Europe and Asia.
2. Communists no longer control this region. Countries are starting free market economies.
3. Plains cover much of the region. The climate is colder than the climate in Western Europe.

◆ Vocabulary

Finish Up   Choose the word or words in dark print that best complete each sentence. Write the word or words on the correct blank line.

> **free market economy**   **command economy**   **continental climate**
> **Commonwealth of Independent States**   **czars**

1. For hundreds of years, kings called ＿＿＿＿＿＿＿＿＿＿＿ ruled Russia.

2. A ＿＿＿＿＿＿＿＿＿＿＿ means there are long, cold winters and short, hot summers.

3. Russia and 11 countries that were part of the Soviet Union are now part of the group called the ＿＿＿＿＿＿＿＿＿＿＿.

4. In a ＿＿＿＿＿＿＿＿＿＿＿, the government decides what factories will make and what workers will earn.

5. In a ＿＿＿＿＿＿＿＿＿＿＿, people own factories, farms, and businesses.

◆ Read and Remember

Write the Answer   Write one or more sentences to answer each question.

1. How did Eastern Europe become a Communist area? ＿＿＿＿＿＿＿＿＿

＿＿＿＿＿＿＿＿＿＿＿＿＿＿＿＿＿＿＿＿＿＿＿＿＿＿＿＿＿＿＿＿

2. How did the Communists not allow people freedom? ＿＿＿＿＿＿＿＿＿

＿＿＿＿＿＿＿＿＿＿＿＿＿＿＿＿＿＿＿＿＿＿＿＿＿＿＿＿＿＿＿＿

3. How did communism end in this region? ＿＿＿＿＿＿＿＿＿＿＿

＿＿＿＿＿＿＿＿＿＿＿＿＿＿＿＿＿＿＿＿＿＿＿＿＿＿＿＿＿＿＿＿

4. What are the main landforms of the region? ＿＿＿＿＿＿＿＿＿＿

＿＿＿＿＿＿＿＿＿＿＿＿＿＿＿＿＿＿＿＿＿＿＿＿＿＿＿＿＿＿＿＿

5. How does the Danube River help Eastern Europe? _____

_____

6. What kinds of climates does the region have? _____

_____

◆ Think and Apply

Categories   Read the words in each group. Decide how they are alike. Find the best title for each group from the words in dark print. Write the title on the line above each group.

**End of Communism   Free Market Economy   Danube River
Command Economy   Natural Resources**

1. _____

government decides what prices to
   charge
government decides what salaries
   to pay
government decides what factories
   will produce

2. _____

people own their own businesses
people decide what factories will
   produce
people decide prices to charge and
   salaries to be paid

3. _____

Poland changed its government
the Berlin Wall was torn down
the Soviet Union broke apart

4. _____

many ports
begins in Germany
flows into the Black Sea

5. _____

coal
iron
oil

◆ Journal Writing

Write a paragraph in your journal that explains how a command economy is different from a free market economy.

CHAPTER 19

Poland: A Changing Industrial Nation

Where Can You Find?

Where can you find some of the oldest salt mines in the world?

Think About As You Read

1. How have Poland's plains helped and hurt the country?
2. How did Solidarity help Poland?
3. Why has it been hard for Poland to have a free market economy?

New Words

- rye
- consumer goods
- concentration camps
- trade unions
- Solidarity
- legal
- privatization
- strike

People and Places

- Czech Republic
- Slovakia
- Ukraine
- Vistula River
- Warsaw
- Gdańsk
- Wieliczka
- Pope John Paul II
- Lech Walesa

Poland is the largest country in Eastern Europe. It is an industrial country. But Poland is different from Western Europe because it is difficult for people to own cars. As you read, find out why fewer than seven million people own cars in Poland.

Poland's Geography and Resources

Most of Poland is covered with plains and rolling hills. In fact the name Poland means "plains." These plains have both helped and hurt Poland. They help Poland by giving the country good farmland. But the flat plains have made it easy for other countries to attack Poland from the east and from the west.

The Baltic Sea is north of Poland. There are many beaches and small lakes near the sea. Mountains are to the south. They separate Poland from three of its neighbors, the Czech Republic, Slovakia, and Ukraine. Look at the map on page 152. Name four other countries that share borders with Poland.

The North European Plain is the largest landform in Poland. What mountains are located in southern Poland?

POLAND

MAP KEY
- • City
- ⊛ Capital city
- –·– Border between countries
- ⁓ River

Poland's flag

A farm in Poland

The Vistula River is the most important river in Poland. It runs from the mountains in the south to the Baltic Sea. This river is used for transportation. Warsaw, Poland's capital and largest city, is on the Vistula River. The port city of Gdańsk is on the Baltic Sea near this river.

Coal is Poland's most important resource. There are rich coal fields in the southern mountains. Poland also has copper, silver, salt, and other resources. Salt mines in Wieliczka are among the oldest in the world. Poland must import two important resources, oil and iron.

People, Culture, and Economy

Almost 39 million people live in Poland. They are called Poles. They speak the Polish language. Very few immigrants from other countries live in Poland.

Religion and education are very important to Poles. Most Poles are Roman Catholics. Pope John Paul II, the world leader of the Catholic Church, grew up in Poland. All children in Poland must go to school for at least nine years. Almost everyone knows how to read and write.

In the past most Poles were farmers. Today only about one fourth of the people work at farming. Potatoes and **rye** are the most important crops. Rye is a grain that is used to make dark bread. These crops grow well in Poland's cool climate.

After World War II, Communist leaders turned Poland into an industrial country. Many factories were built. Now one third of the people work at factory jobs. Polish factories make products such as steel, cement, and machines. But they do not make many **consumer goods**. Consumer goods are things people buy for their own needs. Clothing and cars are two kinds of consumer goods. Many Poles also work at service jobs.

Poland has a lower standard of living than Western Europe. Poles earn low salaries, and consumer goods are expensive. Poles must spend most of their money on food. Fewer than 7 million people own cars. Most city people live in small apartments.

Apartments in Poland

Poland's History

Poland has been conquered many times. In 1795 Germany, Austria, and Russia conquered Poland. The three countries divided Poland. In that year Poland disappeared from the map of Europe. Poland did not become a free nation again until after World War I.

During World War II, Germany and Russia conquered and divided Poland again. The German Army built six **concentration camps**, or death camps, in Poland. Most of Poland's 3 million Jews were killed in those concentration camps during the Holocaust. Three million Christian Poles also died during the war.

After the war, Russia forced Poland to have a Communist government. Most Poles were not happy with their Communist government. Communist leaders made it hard for people to practice the Catholic religion. The Poles wanted the freedom to speak out against their leaders. They also wanted a free market economy.

During World War II, this was a concentration camp in Poland.

In 1980 Polish workers began to form **trade unions**. Trade unions are groups that help workers. Sometimes they help workers get better salaries. All of the new Polish trade unions became part of a group called **Solidarity**. The Communists made it against the law to join Solidarity. Solidarity leaders were sent to jail. But millions of Poles continued to join Solidarity.

Members of Solidarity called for changes in the government and economy of Poland.

Lech Walesa and other Poles can now vote in free elections.

They hoped the unions would bring more freedom to Poland. Lech Walesa became the leader of Solidarity.

In 1989 the government said it was **legal** for people to join Solidarity. That same year Poles voted in the country's first free election. The Communists lost the election. Lech Walesa was elected president.

Poland began to change to a free market economy. The government began the **privatization** of factories. This means the government started selling the factories it owned to private companies.

People have much more freedom in Poland today. But changing to a free market economy has been very difficult. About 6 million people do not have jobs. Food and consumer goods are very expensive.

In 1995 Poles voted in free elections again. This time many Communists were elected to government positions.

The Future of Poland

Today Polish factories make more products than ever before. Poland exports more goods each year. But Poland still has a much lower standard of living than Western Europe. Most factories do not have modern technology. Most farmers do not use modern methods. Poland is trying to buy new technology from Western Europe and the United States. This will help Poland become a more modern country. Many American companies have started businesses in Poland.

Poland wants more friendship with Western Europe. So it is planning to become a member of NATO and the European Union.

Most Poles are unhappy that they still do not have enough consumer goods. They do not like the high prices they must now pay for food and goods. Will Poland become a Communist nation again? Will the country change back to a command economy? The people of Poland still have much work to do.

Poland now has a free market economy.

Chapter Main Ideas

1. Poland's plains have good farmland.
2. Communists lost control of Poland in 1989 when Solidarity leaders were elected in free elections.
3. Poland is trying to have a free market economy. But Poland needs modern technology to improve the standard of living of its people.

BIOGRAPHY

Lech Walesa (Born 1943)

Lech Walesa helped end communism in Poland. He saw how unfair Poland's Communist government was to Polish workers. So he told workers to join trade unions. He helped the unions unite to form Solidarity. Walesa became the leader of Solidarity.

In 1980 Walesa helped the workers win a **strike** against the government. But the government decided that Solidarity was illegal. Walesa was sent to jail. While in jail he won the Nobel Peace Prize for his work for Solidarity.

After Walesa was freed, he continued working to end communism in Poland. In 1989, Poland had its first free elections. Walesa was elected president. Walesa grew less popular when goods became very expensive. Walesa ran for president again and lost. He continues to speak out against communism in Poland.

Journal Writing
Write a paragraph in your journal that tells how Lech Walesa helped end communism in Poland.

◆ Vocabulary

Match Up Finish the sentences in Group A with words from Group B. Write the letter of each correct answer on the blank line.

Group A

1. A grain called _____ is used for making dark bread.

2. Goods that people buy for their own use are _____.

3. Death camps that were built by the German Army during World War II were called _____.

4. Groups that help workers get better salaries are _____.

5. Something that is allowed by law is _____.

6. When the government sells the factories it owns to private companies, there is _____.

Group B

A. trade unions

B. rye

C. legal

D. concentration camps

E. consumer goods

F. privatization

◆ Read and Remember

Finish the Paragraph Use the words in dark print to finish the paragraph below. Write the words you choose on the correct blank lines.

disappeared	**Lech Walesa**	**consumer**	**coal**
Warsaw	**plains**	**Catholic**	

Much of Poland is covered with _____. The capital of Poland,

_____, is on the Vistula River. Poland's most important resource is

_____. Most Poles practice the _____ religion.

Poland is an industrial country, but it manufactures fewer _____

goods than Western Europe. Fewer than 7 million Poles own cars. In 1795, Austria,

Russia, and Germany took control of Poland. Poland _____ from

the map of Europe until after World War I. _____ worked to end

communism in Poland while he was the leader of Solidarity.

◆ Think and Apply

Cause and Effect   Match each cause on the left with an effect on the right.
Write the letter of the effect on the correct blank.

Cause

1. Poland has flat plains, so _____.

2. Three million Jews were killed in the

Holocaust, so today _____.

3. Poland has a cool climate, so _____.

4. After World War II, Poland became

an industrial country, so _____.

5. In 1980 Polish workers wanted better

salaries and more freedom, so _____.

6. Today Poland wants to have a free

market economy, so _____.

Effect

A. farmers grow rye and potatoes

B. there is privatization of factories

C. it has been easy for enemies to
attack Poland

D. there are about 10,000 Jews in
Poland

E. they joined Solidarity

F. fewer people are farmers

◆ Journal Writing

Write a paragraph in your journal that tells how communism ended in Poland.

Understanding Line Graphs

Line graphs are used to show **trends.** Trends are changes that take place over a period of time.

The line graph on this page shows how Poland's imports and exports have changed between 1982 and 1994. Since communism ended in Poland in 1989, the country has had more trade with Western Europe. It has more imports and exports.

Look at the line graph on this page. Then finish each sentence in Group A with an answer from Group B. Write the letter of the correct answer on the blank line.

Group A

1. In 1982 Poland had _____ in exports

2. In _____ Poland's imports were $5.4 billion.

3. In 1990 Poland earned _____ from its exports.

4. Poland exported more than it imported every

year except _____.

5. In 1994 Poland did not have a _____ balance of trade.

Group B

A. 1994

B. $13.5 billion

C. favorable

D. 1986

E. $4.96 billion

CHAPTER 20

Russia: The World's Largest Country

Where Can You Find?
Where can you find frozen rivers used as roads?

Think About As You Read

1. What landforms and climates are in Russia?
2. Why is transportation poor in many parts of Russia?
3. What problems does Russia have today?

New Words

- tundra
- steppes
- Russian Orthodox Church
- republics
- plots
- heavy industries
- glasnost
- shortage
- social problems
- alcohol abuse

People and Places

- Trans-Siberian Railroad
- Moscow
- Siberia
- Volga River
- Kremlin
- St. Petersburg
- Petrograd
- Leningrad
- Mikhail Gorbachev
- Boris Yeltsin
- Chechnya
- Lake Baikal

Imagine traveling across Russia by train. You would board the Trans-Siberian Railroad in Asia near the Pacific Ocean. For six days you would travel west through Russia. After traveling more than 5,000 miles, you would finally reach Moscow, the capital of Russia. You would still have to travel another 1,000 miles to cross the border of the world's largest country.

Russia's Landforms, Climates, and Resources

Russia is almost twice the size of the United States. Russia is on two continents. The western part is in Europe. The eastern part is in Asia and is called Siberia. The Ural Mountains separate Europe and Asia.

Most of Russia has very long, cold winters. It is cold because it is so far north. Snow covers much of the country for at least six months each year. The temperature in January is often below 0°F. As you move south, the climate becomes warmer. The region near the Black Sea has a mild Mediterranean climate.

The Trans-Siberian Railroad crosses Russia, the largest country in the world. Which two cities are connected by the railroad?

Russia's flag

RUSSIA

MAP KEY
- • City
- ⊛ Capital city
- –·– Border between countries
- ⌒ River
- +++++ Trans-Siberian Railroad

A village in Siberia

Most of Russia is covered with plains. Plains cover European Russia west of the Urals. Plains also cover a large part of Siberia east of the Urals. The plains can be divided into three regions. The northern plains are cold and icy. This icy land is called **tundra**. The tundra is covered with permafrost like northern Canada, which you read about in Chapter 3. Only small plants can grow on permafrost in summer. The second region is south of the tundra. Thick forests cover the land. South of the forests are grassy plains called **steppes**. This region has the best farmland in Russia.

Russia has some of the world's longest rivers. At 2,300 miles, the Volga River is the longest river in Europe. In the summer, rivers in Russia are used for shipping and transportation. But most rivers freeze in the winter. Trucks then use the frozen rivers as roads.

Russia has a long northern seacoast. But the water near the coast is filled with ice for many months during the winter. There are few ports that are good for shipping throughout the year. This makes it hard for Russia to trade with other countries.

Russia has more natural resources than any other country in the world. It has coal, oil, and many kinds

St. Petersburg is a port on the Baltic Sea. The city was built on more than 100 islands. Like Venice, this city has many canals.

of metals. But many resources are not being used. Most resources are in Siberia. The cold climate makes them difficult to mine. Also because of the cold, northern Siberia does not have good transportation for moving resources to factories.

Russia's People and Cities

Russia has 148 million people. This is a much smaller population than in the United States. Most Russians live in the European part of Russia. About three fourths of Russia's people live in cities. Russia's largest cities are in the European part of Russia.

Moscow is Russia's capital and its largest city. It has about 10 million people. Moscow is the center of the government and the economy. Russia's leaders meet in the Kremlin in Moscow. The Kremlin includes several buildings surrounded by a wall.

St. Petersburg is Russia's second largest city. It was Russia's capital for 200 years. The city has had two other names, Petrograd and Leningrad.

Russia is a country with more than 100 different ethnic groups. They have different languages and cultures. Most people in European Russia belong to the **Russian Orthodox Church**. There are also many Muslims in parts of Siberia.

This gate is one entrance to the Kremlin in Moscow.

The Soviet Union launched many rockets. Today Russia continues to send rockets into space.

Mikhail Gorbachev

Russia's History

From 1922 until 1991, Russia was part of a larger nation called the Soviet Union. The Soviet Union had 15 **republics**, or states. Russia was the largest and most powerful republic. A Communist government in Moscow ruled the entire nation. The Soviet Union was ruled by dictators.

The Communist leaders controlled the way people farmed. The government, not the people, owned most farms. Farmers were allowed to own very small **plots**, or areas of land. They could only grow crops for their own families on these plots. But one fourth of the nation's crops came from these small private plots.

The Soviet Union became an industrial country. Its Communist government owned all factories and businesses. The government did not allow Soviet factories to make many consumer goods. Instead the factories were used for **heavy industries**. Heavy industries make steel, machines, weapons, and other large products.

Communism helped the Soviet Union become a modern nation. The Communists sent rockets into space. They built a powerful army. People had more food. All children went to free schools. But people had no freedom in the Soviet Union. They could not move from one city to another without permission from the government. People were not allowed to practice their religion. People who spoke out against the Communist government were punished. Many millions were sent to jails in Siberia. Other people were killed. Many people were unhappy living with communism. They wanted more freedom.

In 1985 Mikhail Gorbachev became the Soviet Union's last Communist president. He allowed people to own businesses. Gorbachev also allowed much more freedom. This idea of openness and freedom was called by its Russian name, **glasnost**. With the new glasnost, people also wanted to be free from the control of the Communist leaders in Moscow. Some of the Soviet republics decided to become independent. At

Russia still has shortages of many goods. Here people wait in line to buy bread.

the end of 1991, the Soviet Union fell apart as a nation. Russia and the other republics became independent countries. Boris Yeltsin became Russia's president. Russia was no longer a Communist country.

Russia Today

Now that communism has ended in their country, Russians are enjoying more freedom. Now people can practice their religion. Privatization of stores, factories, and farms is taking place. But Russia has many difficult problems today. Most people earn low salaries. Many people do not have jobs. There is also a **shortage** of housing. There are not enough apartments in the cities for all the people who need them. There are also food shortages. People must stand in line for hours and pay high prices to buy food.

Inflation is another problem. The Communists had kept the prices of certain goods low so all people could buy them. Prices are now very high because the government does not control them. People find it hard to pay for expensive food and clothing.

Health care in Russia is very poor. The country does not have enough medicine to treat sick people.

There are **social problems**, too. There is much crime in Russia. **Alcohol abuse** is another problem. Many Russians drink too many alcoholic drinks.

Boris Yeltsin

The fighting in Chechnya has killed many people and destroyed many buildings.

A city in Chechnya during the fighting

There have also been problems with ethnic groups. In one part of Russia called Chechnya, the people want to have their own independent country. In 1994 they started fighting the Russian Army. They fought for almost two years. The fighting has stopped. No one knows what Chechnya's future will be.

Why are there so many problems in Russia? One reason is that the country does not have modern technology. It needs better technology for its farms, factories, and hospitals. Also Russia does not have enough transportation. Crops often rot in the fields because there is no way to get them to markets. Russia needs better ways to move resources and food.

Today Russia is trying to be a democracy. It is trying to have a free market economy. Russians need a higher standard of living. Then they will be able to enjoy life without communism.

Chapter Main Ideas

1. Plains cover most of Russia. Snow covers most of the country for at least six months of the year.
2. Communism ended in 1991. Since then, there have been food and housing shortages.
3. Siberia has most of Russia's resources. But Russia has not been able to use many of those resources.

Siberia

Siberia is the huge Asian part of Russia. This cold region has three fourths of Russia's land but less than one fifth of its people.

At one time Siberia had many jails. Communist leaders sent people who spoke against the government to those jails. Many people were in Siberian jails for more than twenty years.

There are many long rivers in Siberia that flow into the Arctic Ocean. The Russians have built dams on these rivers. These dams make electricity that is used in western Russia.

Lake Baikal is one of the most interesting places in Siberia. It is the world's deepest freshwater lake. It is more than 6,000 feet deep. Almost 2,000 different kinds of plants and animals live in Lake Baikal. At times the waves in the lake are 15 feet high.

Russia wants to develop Siberia since it has most of the country's natural resources. People who move to work in Siberia are paid salaries that are higher than salaries in other places in Russia.

The Trans-Siberian Railroad has made it easier for people and resources to travel through southern Siberia. Pipelines carry oil and gas to western Russia. But there are few roads and railroads in the north. New ways are needed to reach the rich resources of northern Siberia.

Lake Baikal in Siberia

Write a sentence to answer each question.

1. Place   Why is Lake Baikal an interesting place in Siberia?

_____

2. Movement   How do people and resources move from Siberia to western

Russia? _____

3. Region   What kind of region is Siberia?

_____

◆ Vocabulary

Finish the Paragraph   Use the words in dark print to finish the paragraph below. Write the words you choose on the correct blank lines.

heavy industries　　**tundra**　　**alcohol abuse**
steppes　　　　　　　**plots**　　　**shortage**

　　Northern Siberia is covered with cold icy land called _____.

Southern Siberia has grassy plains called _____. Russia's best

farmland is there. In the past Russian farmers grew crops on small areas of land,

or _____. Russia has become an industrial country. Most Russian

factories manufacture goods like steel, machines, and weapons. These are products

of _____. There are not enough apartments in Russian cities, so

there is a _____ of housing. One big social problem in Russia is

_____, which means people drink too many alcoholic drinks.

◆ Read and Remember

Where Am I?   Read each sentence. Then look at the words in dark print for the name of the place for each sentence. Write the name of the correct place on the blank after each sentence.

Chechnya　　**St. Petersburg**　　**Black Sea**
Moscow　　　**northern Siberia**

1. "I am in a port on the Baltic Sea." _____

2. "I am in Russia's capital." _____

3. "I am at a beach in southern Russia." _____

4. "I am in a region covered with tundra." _____

5. "I am in a region where fighting began in 1994." _____

◆ Think and Apply

Drawing Conclusions   Read each pair of sentences. Then look in the box for the conclusion you might make. Write the letter of the conclusion on the blank.

1. Russia is on two continents.
Russia is almost twice the size of the United States.

Conclusion: _____

2. Snow covers much of Russia for six months each year.
Trucks travel on frozen rivers in the winter.

Conclusion: _____

3. Few people want to work or live in northern Siberia.
There are no railroads in northern Siberia.

Conclusion: _____

4. People who spoke out against the Soviet Union's leaders were sent to jail.
Communist leaders did not allow freedom of religion.

Conclusion: _____

5. There are shortages of housing and food in Russia today.
There are many people who do not have jobs.

Conclusion: _____

Conclusions
A. There was little freedom in the Soviet Union.
B. It has been difficult for Russia to change to a free market economy.
C. Most of Russia has a very cold climate.
D. Russia has not developed the resources of northern Siberia.
E. Russia is a huge country.

◆ Journal Writing

Write a paragraph that tells three ways in which Russia has changed since communism ended.

Reading a Statistics Table

A **table** is a chart that has **statistics**, or numbers, that provide information about a topic. Tables can be used to compare, to contrast, or to draw conclusions. The table below gives statistics for the population and the number of cars in six countries. To read this table, first read the name of each heading. To find information about each heading, read the table from top to bottom. To find information about each country, read the table from left to right.

Read the statistics table. Then use the words in dark print to finish each sentence. Write the answers you choose on the correct blanks.

two	**command economy**	**the United States**	**population**
eight	**smallest**	**largest**	

1. The United States has the _____ population of the six countries.

2. Ukraine has the _____ number of cars.

3. Russia has a larger population than every country on the table except for

_____.

4. Poland and Spain have almost the same _____.

5. Spain has almost _____ times more cars than Poland.

6. France has about _____ times more cars than Ukraine.

7. We can conclude that countries that had a _____ have fewer cars.

The Population and Number of Cars for Six Countries

Country	Population	Number of Cars
Russia	148,200,000	11 million
United States	265,600,000	146 million
Poland	38,600,000	7 million
Spain	39,200,000	13 million
Ukraine	50,800,000	3 million
France	58,000,000	24 million

CHAPTER 21

The Commonwealth of Independent States

Where Can You Find?

Where can you find a large port on the Black Sea?

Think About As You Read

1. Why was the C.I.S. formed?
2. How do C.I.S. countries differ from each other?
3. Why is Ukraine a poor country when it is rich in natural resources?

New Words

- organization
- nuclear weapons
- mosques
- radioactive wastes
- contaminated
- chernozem

People and Places

- Belarus
- Moldova
- Minsk
- Caucasus Mountains
- Caspian Sea
- Georgia
- Armenia
- Azerbaijan
- Central Asia
- Kiev
- Dnepr River
- Odessa
- Chernobyl

Imagine traveling through the 12 countries that are part of the Commonwealth of Independent States, the C.I.S. As you cross the border to go from one nation to another, you must show your passport to the border guards. You have to change your money to the currency of each republic that you visit. You also must know about the laws of each republic. Since the Soviet Union broke apart in 1991, each republic has its own laws, army, money, stamps, and flag.

Understanding the C.I.S.

The C.I.S. is an **organization**, or group, of 12 new countries. These countries had been republics of the Soviet Union. Russia is the largest C.I.S. country. Estonia, Latvia, and Lithuania are three republics that had been part of the Soviet Union, but did not join the C.I.S. These Baltic countries have closer ties with Western Europe than with Russia.

The C.I.S. was formed from 12 countries that had been part of the Soviet Union. What are the two largest countries in the C.I.S.?

THE COMMONWEALTH OF INDEPENDENT STATES

ARCTIC OCEAN

NORWAY

Barents Sea

Bering Sea

Baltic Sea

FINLAND

RUSSIA

ESTONIA
LATVIA
LITHUANIA

BELARUS

S I B E R I A

Sea of Okhotsk

UKRAINE

Volga River

URAL MTS.

Ob River

Yenisey River

RUSSIA

Lena River

MOLDOVA

ARMENIA

Lake Baikal

GEORGIA

Caspian Sea

KAZAKSTAN

AZERBAIJAN

UZBEKISTAN

MONGOLIA

CHINA

TURKMENISTAN

KYRGYZSTAN

IRAN

TAJIKISTAN

MAP KEY
- - - Border between countries
~ River

The C.I.S. was formed in 1991 to help the 12 new countries work together. One goal of the C.I.S. is to improve trade among these countries. Another goal is to control the **nuclear weapons** in this region. These weapons are powerful bombs that can destroy large cities. Russia and three other republics had nuclear weapons. These new nations gave Russia their nuclear weapons. Russia has promised to destroy the weapons.

Three Groups of Nations in the C.I.S.

The twelve C.I.S. countries can be divided into three regions. The first region includes Russia and three countries that are east of Russia—Ukraine, Belarus, and Moldova. Minsk, the capital of Belarus, is also the capital of the C.I.S. These four countries are the most industrial countries in the C.I.S.

The second region includes the three countries in the Caucasus Mountains. They are located between the Black Sea and the Caspian Sea. In two countries, Georgia and Armenia, most people are Orthodox Christians. In the third country, Azerbaijan, most people are Muslims. Georgia and Armenia have good farmland. Azerbaijan has oil, but it has not developed this resource yet.

This mosque is one of many found in Central Asia today.

The third region includes the five countries in Central Asia. In all of these countries, most people are Muslims. They feel closer to the Muslim countries of Asia than to the countries of Europe. There were not many **mosques** in Central Asia when it was part of the Soviet Union. A mosque is where Muslims pray. Since communism has ended, more people practice their religion. There are now thousands of mosques in Central Asia.

Central Asia has a dry climate. Many people work at farming or herding animals. These are the poorest countries of the C.I.S. Some of these countries have oil, but they have not developed that resource.

Each country in the C.I.S. has its own culture. Let's look more closely at Ukraine.

Ukraine: Its Geography, People, and History

Most of Ukraine is covered by the North European Plain. Ukraine has steppes with good farmland. Ukraine, like other countries of this region, has a continental climate. Winters are cold and summers are warm. Ukraine has a warmer climate than Russia. In the south, near the Black Sea, the climate is warmest.

Many people work at herding in Azerbaijan.

About 51 million people live in Ukraine. Two thirds live in cities. Kiev is the capital and the largest city. It is on the Dnepr River. The river is important for transportation and hydroelectric power. Odessa is a large, important port on the Black Sea.

Ukraine has a long history. But for hundreds of years, it was ruled by other countries. Ukraine was one of the first countries forced to become part of the

Ukraine has several large rivers. The Dnepr River flows into the Black Sea. What port city is located on the Black Sea?

Flag of Ukraine

The Chernobyl nuclear power plant

Soviet Union. The Soviet Union tried very hard to turn Ukraine into a Russian country. Only about one fifth of the people are Russians. All schools, television shows, and newspapers had to use the Russian language. But the people of Ukraine kept their own language and culture. In 1991 Ukraine became independent. It joined the C.I.S. that same year. Today Ukrainian is the official language. Many people speak both Ukrainian and Russian.

In 1986 a nuclear power plant in the city of Chernobyl caught on fire and exploded. The power plant was near Kiev. The plant had been built by the Soviet Union. The explosion sent large amounts of **radioactive wastes** into the air, water, and soil. Neighboring countries were polluted with these wastes. Ukrainians said at least 6,000 people died because of the accident. People continue to become sick from wastes in the air, the water, and the soil. The area around Chernobyl is still **contaminated**, or polluted, with these dangerous radioactive wastes.

Ukraine's Resources and Economy

Ukraine is rich in resources. Its fertile black soil is one of its most important resources. This soil, called

chernozem, gives Ukraine some of the best farmland in the world. About one fifth of the people are farmers. The country produces more wheat than any other country in Europe. Farmers also grow corn, rye, potatoes, and sugar beets.

Ukraine also has many minerals. It has large amounts of coal and iron for its industries. One fourth of all manufactured goods in the C.I.S. comes from Ukraine. Factories produce steel, machines, cement, glass, trains, and other products. But they do not make enough consumer goods. Ukraine imports consumer goods from Europe, North America, and Asia. Ukraine has some oil and natural gas. But Ukraine does not have enough for all its needs. It imports oil and natural gas from Russia and other C.I.S. countries. Ukraine trades other goods with Russia and the other C.I.S. nations.

Ukraine is moving toward a free market economy. More and more factories are now owned by private companies. But farms are still owned by the government. There are very few private farms.

Ukraine is rich in resources, but it is a poor country. Ukraine is a poor country because it lacks modern technology. Ukraine's factory products are not as good as those from Western Europe and the United States. Most workers earn only about $2,000 a year. Ukraine is working hard to improve its economy.

No one knows what the future of the C.I.S. will be. Will it become like the European Union and join the countries of the region together? Will the 12 members continue to be part of the C.I.S.? People around the world are watching to see how this region will change.

Ukraine has some of the best farmland in the world.

The people of Ukraine have a long history with many traditions.

Chapter Main Ideas

1. The C.I.S. was formed from countries that had been republics of the Soviet Union.
2. The 12 countries of the C.I.S. include many languages, ethnic groups, and cultures.
3. Ukraine produces large amounts of farm crops and factory goods. More modern technology will help improve Ukraine's economy.

◆ Vocabulary

Finish Up   Choose the word or words in dark print that best complete each sentence. Write the word or words on the correct blank line.

> **nuclear weapon**   **radioactive**   **contaminated**
> **organization**   **mosque**   **chernozem**

1. An atomic bomb is a type of _____.

2. The fertile soil in Ukraine is called _____.

3. The waste products from making nuclear energy are _____ wastes.

4. The C.I.S. is a group, or _____, made from new countries that had been Soviet republics.

5. Water is _____, or not pure, when there are wastes in it.

6. A building where Muslims pray is a _____.

◆ Read and Remember

Write the Answer   Write one or more sentences to answer each question.

1. What are two goals of the C.I.S.? _____

2. Which three republics of the Soviet Union did not join the C.I.S.? _____

3. Which four C.I.S. countries are the most industrial? _____

4. Which group of C.I.S. countries has a large Muslim population? _____

5. What happened at Chernobyl? _____

_____

6. What products does Ukraine manufacture? _____

_____

7. Why is Ukraine a poor country? _____

_____

◆ Think and Apply

Fact or Opinion   Write **F** next to each fact. Write **O** next to each opinion. You should find four sentences that are opinions.

_____ **1.** There are 12 republics in the C.I.S.

_____ **2.** The C.I.S. will fall apart.

_____ **3.** The Baltic countries should join the C.I.S.

_____ **4.** Each republic has its own language, money, laws, and culture.

_____ **5.** The republics of Central Asia have a dry climate.

_____ **6.** Russia has more people than Ukraine.

_____ **7.** Most of Ukraine's trade should be with the C.I.S.

_____ **8.** Ukraine has fertile soil and mineral resources.

_____ **9.** Ukraine farmers should own their own farms.

_____ **10.** The explosion at Chernobyl caused serious pollution problems.

◆ Journal Writing

Imagine you are traveling through the C.I.S. Write a paragraph in your journal that tells which two countries you would visit. Tell why you would visit those countries.

Understanding a Resource Map

Resource maps show where resources can be found in an area. Some resource maps can show where minerals are found. Other maps show where farm and factory products are found. The resource map on this page shows where resources can be found in Ukraine.

Use the map key to find out which resources are shown. Then circle the answer to each question.

1. What resource is near the Donets River?

    coal   iron ore   oil

2. What two resources are found in southern Ukraine?

    natural gas and coal   natural gas and iron ore   coal and oil

3. What resource is not found in western Ukraine?

    coal   iron ore   oil

4. Where can you find natural gas?

    Kharkiv   Donetsk   Odessa

5. What city would have many factories because it is near coal fields?

    Odessa   Donetsk   Kherson

CHAPTER 22

The New Nations of Yugoslavia

Where Can You Find?

Where can you find a city where Olympic Games were played in 1984?

Think About As You Read

1. When did Yugoslavia first become a nation?
2. How did the end of communism change Yugoslavia?
3. Why did Bosnia have a civil war?

New Words

- Islam
- nationalism
- majority
- ethnic cleansing
- cease-fire
- central government

People and Places

- Sarajevo
- Yugoslavia
- Balkan Peninsula
- Croats
- Serbs
- Slovenia
- Croatia
- Serbia
- Montenegro
- Macedonia
- Bosnia and Herzegovina
- Bosnia
- Josip Broz Tito
- Dayton, Ohio

In 1984 many people came to the city of Sarajevo in Yugoslavia to watch and compete in the winter Olympic Games. At that time no one knew that within ten years Sarajevo would be destroyed by war.

The Location of Yugoslavia

The Balkan Peninsula is in southeastern Europe. Greece and several Eastern European countries are on this peninsula. Mountains cover most of the countries on the Balkan Peninsula. Most of this region has a continental climate. People near the coast enjoy sandy beaches and a Mediterranean climate.

Yugoslavia is one of the countries on the Balkan Peninsula. Since 1991 Yugoslavia has been changing. It has also been having a civil war.

Yugoslavia's History

When World War I ended, Europe's leaders created new borders between their countries. In some places they also created new countries. Several small countries were joined together to form Yugoslavia.

177

Four republics became new countries in this region when they left Yugoslavia. What two republics are still in Yugoslavia?

NEW NATIONS OF YUGOSLAVIA

MAP KEY
- ⊛ Capital city
- –·– Border between countries
- — Border between republics
- ∼ River

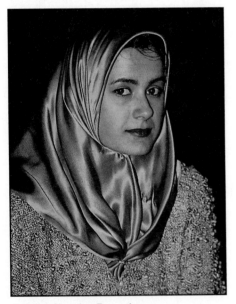

A Muslim in Bosnia

Several ethnic groups lived in these countries. Croats, Serbs, and Muslims were the three largest ethnic groups in Yugoslavia. These groups have lived in this region for hundreds of years. But they have often fought each other. Each group has a different culture and follows a different religion. Croats are Roman Catholics, and Serbs are Orthodox Christians. Muslims follow **Islam**, the world's second largest religion. Today there are more than 1 billion Muslims, mostly in Asia and Africa.

After World War II, Yugoslavia became a Communist country. At that time the country had six states, or republics. They were Slovenia, Croatia, Serbia, Montenegro, Macedonia, and Bosnia and Herzegovina. Bosnia and Herzegovina is often called Bosnia. Josip Broz Tito was Yugoslavia's Communist dictator. Tito forced the different ethnic groups to live together. After Tito died the ethnic groups began fighting again.

Communism ended in Yugoslavia in 1990. Then Croatia, Slovenia, Macedonia, and Bosnia became independent countries. In 1992 only the republics of Serbia and Montenegro remained part of Yugoslavia.

178

Much of Sarajevo has been destroyed because of the civil war in Bosnia.

War in Bosnia

Nationalism soon became a big problem in this region. Nationalism means a very strong love for your country or ethnic group. Nationalism was especially strong in Serbia. That country wanted all Serbs in the region to form a larger Serbian nation. They wanted to control the areas in Bosnia where Serbs lived.

A civil war began in Bosnia in 1992. It became Europe's worst war since World War II. Bosnia's ethnic groups fought to control the country. The Bosnian Serbs fought against the Muslims. The Serbs were angry that Muslims controlled Bosnia's government. Bosnian Croats also fought to control part of the country. Not one of these ethnic groups had a **majority**, or more than half, of Bosnia's people.

During the civil war, Bosnian Serbs captured about two thirds of Bosnia. Serbian soldiers from Yugoslavia helped the Bosnian Serbs. The Serbs removed and often killed all people from other ethnic groups who lived in areas the Serbs had captured. Thousands of people were killed. People have called this **ethnic cleansing**. Some Muslims and Croats also did some ethnic cleansing. Bosnia's ethnic cleansing reminded people of the killing of Jews in the Holocaust.

Leaders in France, Great Britain, Russia, and other European countries tried to end the war. They met

Ethnic Groups in Bosnia

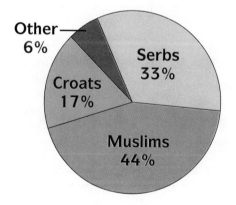

Other 6%
Croats 17%
Serbs 33%
Muslims 44%

NATO soldiers from Great Britain help carry out the peace plan in Bosnia.

with leaders from Bosnia, Croatia, and Serbia. These leaders agreed to a **cease-fire**, an agreement to stop fighting. But the fighting started again.

In 1995 the United States helped end the civil war. The leaders of Bosnia, Croatia, and Serbia met in Dayton, Ohio. They agreed to divide Bosnia into two states. Bosnian Muslims and Croats control one state. Bosnian Serbs control the other state. Each state has its own government. A **central government** in Sarajevo leads all of Bosnia. The government in Sarajevo is led by a Muslim, a Croat, and a Serb. These leaders take turns working as president of Bosnia.

Leaders in the United States and Western Europe feared that fighting could begin again in Bosnia. So they sent 60,000 NATO soldiers to Bosnia to carry out the peace plan. Thousands of American soldiers were sent to Bosnia in 1996. So far, NATO soldiers have kept peace in Bosnia.

Looking at Bosnia's Future

Bosnia's long civil war destroyed much of the country. The war destroyed much of Sarajevo and other cities. Many factories, farms, roads, and railroads are gone. Before 1990 many tourists visited Yugoslavia and its neighbors each year. The region no longer earns money from tourism.

The Bosnians have begun to rebuild their country. They are slowly returning to work. Yugoslavia, Bosnia, and Croatia have many natural resources that could help their people have a higher standard of living.

The ethnic groups of this region continue to hate each other. Will people in Bosnia live in peace after NATO soldiers return home? Will another civil war begin? No one knows what Bosnia's future will be.

Children in Bosnia have gone back to school now that the civil war has ended.

Chapter Main Ideas

1. Yugoslavia was created after World War I.
2. Communism ended in Yugoslavia in 1990. Four republics became independent countries. By 1992 only Serbia and Montenegro were part of Yugoslavia.
3. Bosnia's three ethnic groups fought a long civil war.

◆ Vocabulary

Match Up   Finish the sentences in Group A with words from Group B. Write the letter of each correct answer on the blank line.

Group A

1. Muslims follow the religion of _____.

2. An agreement to stop fighting is a _____.

3. The main government that has control over

other governments in a country is the _____.

4. A strong love for your nation or ethnic group

is _____.

Group B

A. Islam

B. central government

C. nationalism

D. cease-fire

◆ Read and Remember

Complete the Geography Organizer   Complete the geography organizer below with information about the new nations of Yugoslavia.

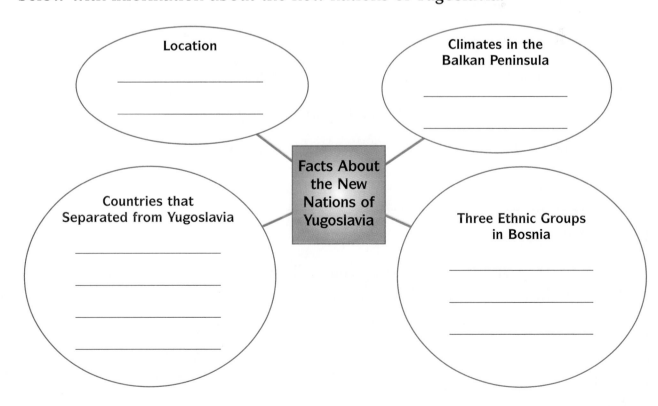

Location

Climates in the Balkan Peninsula

Facts About the New Nations of Yugoslavia

Countries that Separated from Yugoslavia

Three Ethnic Groups in Bosnia

Matching   Each item in Group B tells about an item in Group A. Write the letter of each item in Group B next to the correct answer in Group A.

Group A

_____ **1.** These people live in Croatia and are Roman Catholics.

_____ **2.** Yugoslavia and Greece are located on this part of southeastern Europe.

_____ **3.** He was the Communist dictator of Yugoslavia after World War II.

_____ **4.** By 1992 only Montenegro and this republic remained part of Yugoslavia.

_____ **5.** The 1984 Olympic Games were held in this city, but now the city has been destroyed by civil war.

Group B

A. Sarajevo

B. Balkan Peninsula

C. Croats

D. Serbia

E. Josip Broz Tito

◆ Think and Apply

Sequencing   Write the numbers **1, 2, 3, 4,** and **5** next to these sentences to show the correct order.

_____ Yugoslavia became a Communist nation after World War II.

_____ Yugoslavia became a nation after World War I.

_____ NATO troops went to Bosnia to carry out the peace plan.

_____ In 1992 a civil war began between Bosnia's ethnic groups.

_____ Leaders of Bosnia, Croatia, and Serbia signed a peace plan in Dayton, Ohio.

◆ Journal Writing

Write a paragraph in your journal that tells why Bosnia's civil war began. Then tell how the United States helped to end the war.

Comparing Historical Maps

A **historical map** shows how a region looked during a certain period of history. You can learn how a region changes over time by comparing two maps of the same place from different time periods. The historical map on the left shows Yugoslavia in 1945. It had six republics at that time. The map on the right shows Yugoslavia in 1992. In that year it had only two republics.

Study and compare the maps. Then use the words in dark print to finish the sentences.

Romania	**Croatia**	**Serbia**
Hungary	**Albania**	**Adriatic Sea**

1. The two republics of Yugoslavia in 1992 were Montenegro and _____.

2. A country that was west of Yugoslavia in 1992 was _____.

3. A country that was south of Yugoslavia in 1945 and 1992 was _____.

4. A country that was north of Yugoslavia in 1945 and 1992 was _____.

5. A country that was east of Yugoslavia in 1945 and 1992 was _____.

6. Yugoslavia had a larger border on the _____ in 1945.

CHAPTER 23

Looking at Eastern Europe and Russia and Its Neighbors

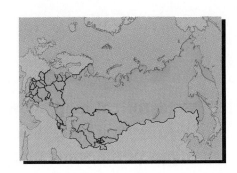

Where Can You Find?
Where can you find a large sea that grows smaller each year?

Think About As You Read

1. What changes have taken place in this region since communism ended?
2. How can nations solve the problems of shortages and not enough technology?
3. How has pollution hurt this region?

New Words

- criticize
- political unrest
- birth defects
- irrigate

People and Places

- Bulgaria
- Hungary
- Aral Sea

Think of the many ways Eastern Europe and Russia and its neighbors have changed since communism ended. Newspapers now have articles that **criticize**, or complain about, the governments. Churches are filled with people on Sunday mornings. People are enjoying more freedom than ever before. But the countries in this region must solve six big problems so that people can have better lives.

Low Standards of Living, Many Shortages, and Not Enough Technology

There are six major problems in this region. The first problem is that most people in this huge region have a low standard of living. In many places people are poorer today than they were under communism. Governments no longer control the price of food and other goods. So products have become more expensive. People are forced to spend more of their money on the food they need.

Farmers in Bulgaria grow good crops, but they do not earn much money.

Some countries are much poorer than others. In Bulgaria many people earn only about $30 a month. In Poland workers may earn more than $300 a month. This is still much less money than an American worker would earn. Poland, Hungary, and the Czech Republic have the highest standards of living in the region. But people in these countries do not live as well as people in Western Europe.

The second problem is shortages. There are not enough apartments for all the people. Most countries do not have enough food. There are shortages of consumer goods because factories do not make enough of them. Communist governments had forced most factories to produce weapons and machines. Today these factories are producing more clothing and consumer goods. But there are still not enough goods for people who have money to buy them.

Shortages are a problem in this region. Shoppers in Budapest, Hungary, wait to buy goods.

Trade is helping the region get more consumer goods. Countries are importing consumer goods from Western Europe, Canada, the United States, and countries in Asia.

A third problem is the need for modern machines and new technology. Many people still use animals for farm work and transportation. Natural resources in Russia and in C.I.S. countries are wasted by old

Political unrest continues to be a problem in this region. Here 50,000 people speak out against their government in Serbia.

machines and old technology. To solve this problem, some countries are importing new technology.

Ethnic Problems, Pollution, and Political Unrest

Fighting between the different ethnic groups in a country is the fourth problem. In Chapter 22 you learned how fighting between ethnic groups in Bosnia led to a terrible civil war. In Russia and in the C.I.S., there have been many fights between ethnic groups. This problem can lead to more civil wars.

Political unrest is the fifth problem. Political unrest means people want to change their governments. After communism ended, countries held free elections. They elected people who were not Communists to lead their governments. But shortages and low standards of living have made people unhappy with their new governments. In some countries, such as Poland and Russia, many Communists have won elections to important government jobs again. Will Communist governments win control of many countries again? No one knows what will happen.

The last problem is the terrible pollution in this region. The Communist governments of Eastern Europe and the Soviet Union had tried to produce a lot of weapons, steel, and factory goods as fast as possible. So they did not care when factories sent pollution into the air. They allowed large amounts of waste to be dumped into rivers and seas. They chopped down forests and

Air pollution from industry is a big problem in this region.

did not plant new trees. So deforestation is a problem in many places.

Today air and water pollution are big problems in this region. A large number of children are born with problems, or **birth defects**, because of the pollution. The water of the Danube River is very polluted. In Russia's large city St. Petersburg, it is not healthy to drink the water. It is not even safe to take baths in St. Petersburg's water. Pollution problems are growing worse.

The Soviet Union hurt the environment near the Aral Sea in Central Asia. The Russians stopped river water from flowing into the Aral Sea. They used the river water to **irrigate** dry desert fields to produce crops. They grew cotton on those fields. Since the rivers did not flow into the Aral Sea, the sea became much smaller. Many plants and animals in the region have died. The desert around the sea has grown larger.

Ships are left in the desert sand as the Aral Sea gets smaller.

Looking at the Future

Eastern Europe and Russia and its neighbors is a region of rich resources. The nations are trying to use their resources to develop modern farms and factories. These countries have worked hard to change to free market economies. They are trying to allow more freedom. It will take time to solve the many problems. But if democracy continues in this region, people everywhere will enjoy a better life.

Chapter Main Ideas

1. Since communism ended, people are enjoying more freedom.
2. Countries changed to free market economies. This led to lower standards of living and many shortages.
3. Communists allowed factories to pollute the air and the water.

Pollution in this region hurts everyone.

◆ Vocabulary

Finish Up   Choose the word or words in dark print that best complete each sentence. Write the word or words on the correct blank line.

political unrest   birth defects   criticize   irrigate

1. To bring water to dry land is to _____ the land.

2. Pollution has caused some babies to be born with problems, or

_____ .

3. When many people want to change the government, there is

_____ .

4. When you find fault with a government, you may _____ it.

◆ Read and Remember

Find the Answer   Put a check (✔) next to each sentence that tells about a problem in Eastern Europe, Russia, and the C.I.S. You should check six sentences.

_____ **1.** The region has a low standard of living.

_____ **2.** There are shortages of food and consumer goods.

_____ **3.** American companies have started businesses in some parts of Eastern Europe.

_____ **4.** Eastern Europe is importing consumer goods from Western Europe.

_____ **5.** There are many fights between ethnic groups.

_____ **6.** Newspapers can criticize the governments.

_____ **7.** Countries do not have modern machines and new technology.

_____ **8.** There is political unrest in some countries in the region.

_____ **9.** Communist governments have damaged the environment.

_____ **10.** Some countries are importing new technology.

Find the Main Idea   Read the five sentences below. Choose the main idea and write it in the main idea box. Then find three sentences that support the main idea. Write them in the boxes of the main idea chart. There will be one sentence in the group that you will not use.

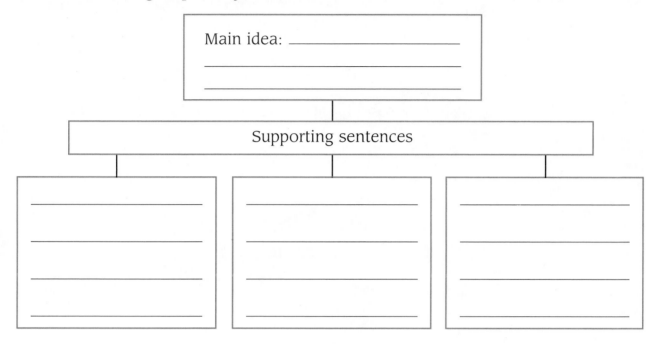

Main idea: _____

Supporting sentences

a. Factories dump wastes into the rivers and seas.

b. Eastern Europe and Russia and its neighbors have terrible pollution problems.

c. It is not safe to drink the water in many cities.

d. There is a shortage of apartments in Russia.

e. Factories send pollution into the air.

◆ **Journal Writing**

Eastern Europe and Russia and its neighbors have many problems. Choose two problems and write a paragraph about them in your journal. Then tell how people might solve the problems.

PACIFIC OCEAN

AUSTRALIA

Darling River

ASIA

Chang Jiang

Huang He

HIMALAYAS

Ganges River

Indus River

Brahmaputra

URAL MOUNTAINS

Arabian Sea

INDIAN OCEAN

EUROPE

ALPS

Danube River

Mediterranean Sea

ARCTIC OCEAN

Nile River

AFRICA

SAHARA DESERT

Congo River

ATLANTIC OCEAN

ANTARCTICA

ATLANTIC OCEAN

NORTH AMERICA

APPALACHIAN MOUNTAINS

ROCKY MOUNTAINS

Mississippi River

Gulf of Mexico

Caribbean Sea

SOUTH AMERICA

Amazon River

ANDES

PACIFIC OCEAN

Bering Sea

Equator

N
E
S
W

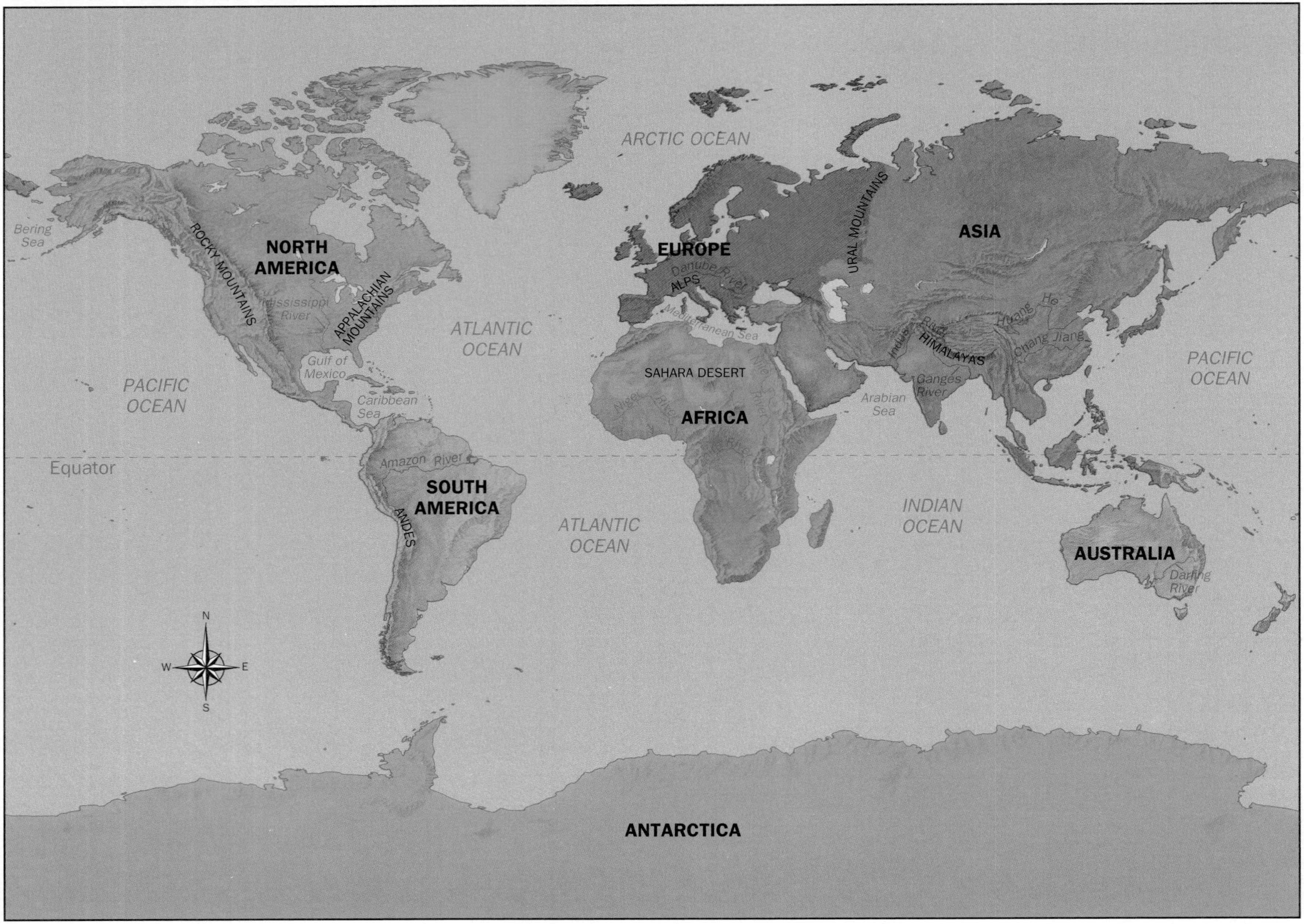

GLOSSARY

acid rain (page 35)   Acid rain forms when pollution in the air becomes part of the rain or snow.

Act of Union (page 106)   The Act of Union joined England, Wales, and Scotland into one nation in 1707.

agriculture (page 100)   Agriculture is another name for farming, growing crops, and raising livestock.

alcohol abuse (page 163)   Alcohol abuse means people drink too many alcoholic drinks.

aluminum (page 66)   Aluminum is a lightweight, shiny metal made from bauxite.

ambassador (page 83)   An ambassador is a representative of his or her government in another country.

arch (page 132)   An arch is a curved opening in doors, bridges, or tunnels.

basin (page 74)   A basin is the area of land that drains into a river.

bauxite (page 66)   Bauxite is an ore used to make aluminum.

Berlin Wall (page 122)   The Berlin Wall separated East Berlin and West Berlin.

birth defect (page 187)   A birth defect is a problem of the mind or body with which some babies are born.

British Commonwealth (page 28)   The British Commonwealth is a group of nations once ruled by Great Britain.

bullet train (page 114)   A bullet train travels faster than 180 miles an hour.

café (page 115)   A café is a sidewalk restaurant popular in France.

calypso (page 66)   Calypso is a type of music that mixes African, Spanish, and American cultures in the Caribbean area.

canal (page 36)   A canal is a human-made waterway dug across land to join two bodies of water.

Carnaval (page 73)   Carnaval is a holiday in Brazil that is celebrated with costumes and parades.

cash crop (page 17)   A cash crop is a crop that can be sold, especially a crop that is exported.

cease-fire (page 180)   A cease-fire is an agreement to stop fighting.

central government (page 180)   The central government is the main government in a country that has other parts with governments, such as states.

chancellor (page 122)   Chancellor is the title of the leader of Germany.

chernozem (page 173)   Chernozem is rich, fertile, black soil in the Ukraine.

citizen (page 15)   A citizen is a member of a country.

civil war (page 58)   During a civil war, people of the same country fight against each other.

climate (page 10)   Climate is the kind of weather a place usually has over a period of time.

coastal plain (page 9)   A coastal plain is flat land near an ocean.

coca (page 82)   Coca is a plant grown to make cocaine.

cocaine (page 82)   Cocaine is an illegal drug made from the coca plant.

colony (page 48)   A colony is land that is ruled by another nation.

command economy (page 146)   In a command economy, the government controls everything and decides what factory products to make, what prices to charge, what wages to pay, and what crops to grow.

Commonwealth of Independent States (CIS) (page 144)   The CIS is an organization of Russia and 11 other former Soviet Union republics.

communism (page 92)   Under communism the government owns and controls all of a country's farms, factories, businesses, and money.

Communist (page 58)   Under a Communist system, the government controls everything in a nation.

concentration camp (page 153) Concentration camps were death camps built by the Germans during World War II to kill Jews and other minorities.

constitutional monarchy (page 100) A constitutional monarchy is a democracy that has a king or queen with little power.

consumer good (page 153) A consumer good is something people buy to eat or to use.

contaminated (page 172) Contaminated means not pure or polluted with something undesirable.

continent (page 4)   A continent is a large body of land on Earth.

continental climate (page 148)   In a continental climate, winters are long and cold. Summers are short and hot.

criticize (page 184)   To criticize is to complain about or to find fault with something.

culture (page 1)   Culture is the beliefs, ideas, art, and customs of a group of people.

currency (page 123)   Currency is the money used by a country.

czar (page 145)   Czars were the kings of Russia before the Russian Revolution.

defeat (page 121)   To defeat means to win a fight.

deforestation (page 75)   Deforestation is the act of destroying a forest by cutting down and burning trees.

democracy (page 10)   In a democracy the people vote for their leaders in free elections.

democratic (page 60)   Democratic means a way of doing things that gives people freedom.

developed nation (page 12) A developed nation is an industrial nation with a high standard of living.

developing nation (page 43) A developing nation has a low standard of living and poor industry or technology.

dictator (page 58)   A dictator has full power to make laws and control a country's land and money.

drug trafficker (page 82)   A drug trafficker ships illegal drugs into countries where the illegal drugs are sold.

earthquake (page 56)   During an earthquake the ground shakes and often cracks open.

Eastern Hemisphere (page 67)   The Eastern Hemisphere is the half of Earth with Europe, Asia, Africa, and Australia.

elevation (page 42)   Elevation tells how high land is above sea level.

empire (page 81)   An empire is a group of nations that is ruled by one country under one leader.

Equator (page 41)   The Equator is the 0° line of latitude that divides the globe into north and south.

ethnic cleansing (page 179)   Ethnic cleansing occurred in Bosnia when the people of one ethnic group removed and killed people from other ethnic groups.

ethnic group (page 106)   An ethnic group is a group of people of the same culture.

euro (page 140)   The euro will be the currency of the European Union in 1999.

European Community (page 140) The European Community was formed by countries of Western Europe to work together to improve trade.

European Union (page 140) The European Union, or EU, is a trade group of 15 European countries.

export (page 33)   To export is to sell goods to other countries.

favorable balance of trade (page 132) A favorable balance of trade means a country exports more than it imports.

fertile (page 98)   Soil that is fertile is good for farming.

fertilizer (page 100)   A fertilizer is a mixture of materials that makes soil better for growing plants.

freedom of religion (page 10) Freedom of religion means people can pray any way and any place they choose.

free market economy (page 147) In a free market economy, citizens and companies own and control factories, farms, and businesses.

geography (page 1)   Geography is the study of Earth's people, landforms, climates, and resources.

geothermal energy (page 139) Geothermal energy uses steam from hot places inside the earth to do work.

glasnost (page 162)   Glasnost is the Russian word for the idea of openness and freedom begun by Mikhail Gorbachev.

heavy industries (page 162) Heavy industries make machines, steel, weapons, and other large products.

highlands (page 56)   Highlands are hills and low mountains.

Holocaust (page 124)   The Holocaust was the German killing of Jews and other people in concentration camps during World War II.

homeless (page 76)   A person who is homeless does not have a place to live.

human/environment interaction
(page 2)   Human/environment interaction is the geography theme that tells how people use, change, and work with a place.

hurricane (page 65)   A hurricane is a tropical storm with very strong winds and heavy rain.

hydroelectric power (page 139) Hydroelectric power is electricity made using the power of falling water.

illegal drug (page 51)   An illegal drug is a substance of which the use and sale are against the law.

illegal immigrant (page 50)   An illegal immigrant is a person who moves into a country without permission.

illiteracy (page 90)   Illiteracy means people cannot read and write.

immigrant (page 10)   An immigrant is a person who moves into a country from another country.

import (page 33)   To import is to buy goods from other countries.

independent (page 66)   Independent means people rule themselves.

industrial nation (page 11)   An industrial nation has factories that use modern technology to make things.

Industrial Revolution (page 106) The Industrial Revolution changed industry from making things by hand at home to making them using machines in factories.

inflation (page 58)   Inflation means goods are more expensive to buy.

interior (page 74)   The interior is the inside, often undeveloped, area of a country away from the borders or coast.

irrigate (page 187)   To irrigate means to bring water to fields.

Islam (page 178)   Islam is the world's second largest religion, practiced mostly in Asia, Africa, and the Middle East.

isthmus (page 59)   An isthmus is a narrow piece of land that is between two large bodies of water.

landform (page 3)   A landform is the shape of an area on Earth's surface. Plains, plateaus, hills, and mountains are the four main landforms.

land reform (page 89)   Land reform occurs when a government divides large plantations into smaller farms that are given to poor farmers.

Latin (page 40)   Latin is a language that few people speak today. The Spanish and Portuguese languages came from Latin.

latitude (page 2)   Lines of latitude are imaginary lines that run east to west and measure distance in degrees north or south of the Equator.

lava (page 56)   Lava is melted rock that pours out from a volcano.

legal (page 154)   Something that is legal is allowed by law.

location (page 2) Location is the geography theme that tells where a place is located, such as near another place. Lines of latitude and longitude give the exact location of a place.

logging (page 26)   Logging is cutting down trees in a forest.

longitude (page 2)   Lines of longitude are imaginary lines that meet at the North and South Pole and measure distance in degrees east or west of the Prime Meridian.

lower class (page 50)   The lower class is a group of poor people who often live in small, poorly made homes in slums or rural villages.

lowlands (page 26)   Lowlands are low, flat land usually near lakes or oceans.

majority (page 179)   A majority means more than half.

manufacture (page 114) To manufacture means to make something from raw materials usually in a factory using machinery.

manufactured goods (page 33) Manufactured goods are goods that are made in factories from other materials.

marijuana (page 84)   Marijuana is a plant that is used as an illegal drug.

Mediterranean climate (page 112) The Mediterranean climate has long, hot, dry summers and short, rainy winters.

mestizo (page 42)   A mestizo is a person in Latin America who has European and Indian ancestors.

middle class (page 50)   The middle class is a group of people who are not rich and not poor.

monarch (page 106)   A monarch is a king or a queen.

monument (page 133)   A monument is a structure built to remember an important person or event.

mosque (page 171)   A mosque is a place of the Islam religion where Muslims pray.

mountain chain (page 9)   A mountain chain is a long group of mountains, the landform with high elevation, often with steep, rocky sides.

mountainous (page 130)   Mountainous means mountains cover a large part of a region.

mouth (page 72)   The mouth of a river is where the river flows into an ocean.

movement (page 2)   Movement is the geography theme that tells how and why people, ideas, and goods move from place to place.

mulatto (page 73)   A mulatto is a person with black African and white European ancestors.

NAFTA (page 34)   NAFTA is the North American Free Trade Agreement between the United States, Canada, and Mexico to improve trade.

national anthem (page 121) A national anthem is a special song that expresses love or pride for one's country.

national debt (page 50)   A country's national debt is the money that it has borrowed and must repay.

nationalism (page 179)   Nationalism means a very strong love or pride for a person's country or ethnic group.

NATO (page 137)   NATO is the North Atlantic Treaty Organization formed by 13 Western European nations, Canada, Turkey, and the United States to protect these countries from communism.

natural gas (page 105)   Natural gas is a natural resource that is used as fuel.

natural resource (page 16)   A natural resource is something in nature that people use such as coal, oil, natural gas, minerals, fish, farmland, and forests.

newsprint (page 26)   Newsprint is paper made from wood and used for making newspapers.

Northern Hemisphere (page 41) The Northern Hemisphere is the half of Earth north of the Equator.

nuclear energy (page 114)   Nuclear energy is derived from uranium and is used to generate electricity.

nuclear power plant (page 114) A nuclear power plant is used to generate electricity from nuclear energy.

nuclear weapon (page 170)   A nuclear weapon is a powerful bomb that can destroy a large city.

ocean current (page 98)   An ocean current is a strong movement of water in the ocean.

official language (page 8)   An official language is the legal language used for all the business of a country.

one-crop economy (page 91)   In a one-crop economy, a country earns most of its money from one crop.

organization (page 169) An organization is a group that joins together for a specific purpose.

oxygen (page 75)   Oxygen is a gas released by plants that most animals need to breathe.

Parliament (page 28)   Parliament is the name of a group of lawmakers in certain democracies.

Partnership for Peace (page 138) The Partnership for Peace, or PfP, is formal cooperation between NATO and former Communist countries in Eastern Europe.

passport (page 137)   A passport is a document given by a government to citizens of that country so they can travel to other countries.

peninsula (page 96)   A peninsula is land that has water on three sides.

permafrost (page 25)   Permafrost is the layer of Arctic and subarctic soil that is always frozen.

petroleum (page 105)   Petroleum is another name for oil.

place (page 2)   Place is the geography theme that tells how an area is different from other areas.

plantation (page 43)   A plantation is a huge farm, especially in the tropics, that grows cash crops such as bananas, coffee, and sugarcane.

plateau (page 3)   A plateau is a broad area of high, flat land. It is one of the four basic landforms.

plot (page 162)   A plot is an area of land, usually small, used for farming.

political unrest (page 186)   During political unrest, people are unhappy with their government and want to change it.

pollution (page 35)   Pollution is waste materials, such as smoke, dirt, trash, and chemicals, that make air and water impure, or not clean.

pope (page 133)   The pope is the world leader of the Roman Catholic Church and the ruler of Vatican City.

population density (page 16) Population density tells how crowded a place is based on the number of people living in a certain size region.

poverty (page 76)   Poverty is the condition of being very poor with a very low standard of living.

prime minister (page 28)   The prime minister is one type of leader of the government in a democracy.

privatization (page 154)   Under privatization a government sells farms and factories it owns to citizens.

province (page 24)   A province is a part of a nation, similar to a state, that has its own government.

Quechua (page 81)   Quechua is an Indian language that is one of the two official languages of Peru.

radioactive waste (page 172) Radioactive waste is contaminated materials left after making nuclear energy.

rapid population growth (page 89) Rapid population growth means the population grows a lot each year.

raw material (page 97)   Raw material is natural resources used to make manufactured products.

recycle (page 139)   To recycle means to use again for the same or a different purpose.

region (page 2)   Region is the geography theme that describes areas based on the area's climate, landforms, culture, or something else in common.

religion (page 1)   Religion is the way people believe and pray to God or to many gods.

republic (page 162)   A republic is a state or nation that is not ruled by a monarch.

revolution (page 106)   A revolution is a dramatic, sudden change.

ruins (page 133)   Ruins are the damaged remains of very old human-made structures.

rural (page 49)   Rural areas are places that are in the countryside, not near a city.

Russian Orthodox Church (page 161) The Russian Orthodox Church is the religion of many European Russians.

Russian Revolution (page 145) The Russian Revolution was the revolt in 1917 of the Russian people against the czar when Communists won control.

rye (page 152)   Rye is a grain that grows well in a cool climate. It is used to make a dark bread.

sea level (page 42)   Sea level, or the ocean surface, is the zero point for measuring the elevation of land.

service job (page 18)   A service job is a job, such as teacher, doctor, clerk, or waiter, where people help other people.

shortage (page 163)   A shortage exists when there is not enough of something, such as food or houses, for all the people who want it.

slum (page 50)   A slum is an area in or around a city where poor people live crowded together in small, poorly made homes.

social problem (page 163)   A social problem is a problem, such as illiteracy, poverty, crime, or pollution, that is caused by and affects people.

solar energy (page 139)   Solar energy uses energy from the sun to do work.

Solidarity (page 153)   Solidarity was an organization of Polish trade unions. Now it is a political party led by Lech Walesa.

Southern Hemisphere (page 41)   The Southern Hemisphere is the half of Earth south of the Equator with Australia, Antarctica, and parts of Africa and South America.

standard of living (page 11) The standard of living measures how well people in a region live.

steel (page 100)   Steel is a strong metal made from iron.

steppes (page 160)   The steppes are grassy plains. Steppes usually have fertile farmland.

strike (page 155)   In a strike, workers refuse to do their jobs until they get what they want such as more money or better working conditions.

subsistence farmer (page 43) A subsistence farmer works on a small farm, growing just enough food for the farmer's own family with nothing left over to sell.

suburb (page 11)   A suburb is a neighborhood close to a city.

tariff (page 34)   A tariff is a tax that is paid on imported goods making them more expensive.

technology (page 18)   Technology is new knowledge, inventions, tools, and skills to help people live or work better.

territory (page 24)   A territory is a place ruled by another nation, but it is not a full part of that nation.

terrorism (page 83)   Terrorism is the use of dangerous acts against the people of a country.

terrorist (page 83)   A terrorist is a person who uses dangerous acts against the people of a country.

theme (page 2)   A theme is an important main idea. There are five themes of geography: location, place, human/environment interaction, movement, and region.

tortillas (page 49)   A tortilla is a flat bread made from corn or wheat.

tourism (page 65)   Tourism is an industry that serves the needs of visitors, such as in hotels, restaurants, and stores.

tourist (page 47)   A tourist is a person who visits a place for pleasure and fun.

trade union (page 153)   A trade union helps workers get better salaries and better working conditions.

traditional (page 49)   Traditional means doing something the same way it has been done in the past.

tropical climate (page 41)   A tropical climate is a climate near the Equator. It is hot all the time with a lot of rain.

tropical rain forest (page 42) A tropical rain forest is a thick forest that grows near the Equator where the climate is very hot and very wet.

tropical storm (page 65)   A tropical storm is a type of storm with heavy rains and strong winds that occurs in the tropics.

tropics (page 41)   The tropics is a region located near the Equator. The tropics has a very hot, rainy tropical climate.

tundra (page 160)   The tundra is far northern plains with cold icy soil covered with permafrost.

unemployment (page 116) Unemployment means people do not have jobs.

unguarded border (page 12) There are no soldiers along an unguarded border.

unification (page 123)   Unification is the act of joining separate parts into one country.

university (page 116)   A university is a type of school that people can go to after they finish high school.

upper class (page 50)   The upper class is a small group of rich people who own most of the land, businesses, and money.

uranium (page 114)   Uranium is a mineral used to make nuclear energy.

urban (page 11)   An urban area is in the city or suburbs, not in the country.

variety (page 15)   Variety means many different kinds, usually at the same time or place.

waterway (page 26)   A waterway is a place, such as a river or a canal, where ships can travel carrying people or materials.

Western Hemisphere (page 67) The Western Hemisphere is the half of Earth with North and South America.

world power (page 107)   A world power is a nation that is an important leader among all countries.

INDEX

acid rain, 35, 139

Africa, 5, 57, 66, 67, 97, 99, 116, 137, 178

Alaska, 9, 10, 15, 17

Algeria, 116

Alps, 98, 113, 123, 130, 131

Amazon River, 39, 41, 44, 72

Amazon River basin, 74

Andes Mountains, 41, 72, 80–84

Antarctica, 5

Apennine Mountains, 130

Aral Sea, 187

Arctic, 10, 25, 27

Arctic Ocean, 5, 9, 24, 97, 165

Aristide, Jean-Bertrand, 68

Armenia, 170

Asia, 5, 18, 67, 81, 97, 99, 116, 137, 144, 147, 159, 178

Atlantic Ocean, 2, 5, 9, 26, 36, 59, 64, 72, 73, 97, 98, 104, 112

Australia, 5, 67

Austria, 153

Azerbaijan, 170, 171

Aztec, 39, 48, 52

Baikal, Lake, 143, 165

balance of trade, 132

Baltic Sea, 97, 123, 144, 151, 152

Belarus, 170

Belgium, 139

Belize, 57

Berlin, Germany, 121–122, 124

Berlin Wall, 122, 124, 146

Black Sea, 148, 159, 170, 171

Bolivia, 80, 84

Bosnia, 178, 179–180, 186

Brasília, Brazil, 2–3, 4, 74

Brazil, 2, 3, 42, 72–76, 92

Budapest, Hungary, 143

Bulgaria, 185

Canada, 7–12, 15, 24–29, 33–36, 103, 138, 147

Canadian Shield, 26

Caribbean Islands, 64–68

Caribbean Sea, 40, 42, 56, 64, 84

Caspian Sea, 170

Castro, Fidel, 67

Caucasus Mountains, 170

Central America, 39, 40–41, 42, 56–60

Central Plateau, 47–48, 52

Chamorro, Violeta Barrios de, 58

Chechnya, 164

Chernobyl, Ukraine, 172

Chile, 83–84, 92

Colombia, 82, 84, 91, 92

Columbus, Christopher, 66

command economy, 146

Commonwealth of Independent States (C.I.S.), 144, 146, 147, 169–173, 185–186

communism, 58, 66–67, 92, 121–122, 125, 145–146, 153–154, 155, 162–163, 165, 178, 186

continental climate, 148, 171, 177

continents, 4–5

Corsica, 112

Costa Rica, 59

Croatia, 178, 180

Croats, 178–180

Cuba, 58, 66–67, 91, 92

currency, 123, 140, 169

Czech Republic, 151, 185

Danube River, 147–148

Dominican Republic, 66, 68

drugs, illegal, 51, 82, 84, 92

earthquakes, 56–57

Eastern Europe, 138, 143–158, 177–189

East Germany, 121–123, 125, 146

Elizabeth, Queen, 103, 106

El Salvador, 58, 90

England, 103, 104–106, 108

English Channel, 103, 104, 108, 112

Equator, 41–42

Erie, Lake, 35

Estonia, 144, 169

Europe, 5, 10, 18, 42, 66, 67, 95–140, 143–159, 177–189

European Union (EU), 140, 155

France, 10, 27–28, 96, 100, 108, 112–116, 121, 130, 139, 179
free market economy, 147, 154, 164, 173
Fujimori, Alberto, 83

Georgia, 170
geothermal energy, 139
Germany, 96, 100, 113, 115, 120–125, 153
Gorbachev, Mikhail, 162
Great Britain, 10, 28, 96, 100, 103, 106–107, 121, 179
Great Lakes, 9, 17, 26, 35, 36
Great Plains, 17, 26–27
Greece, 129, 130, 139, 177
Guatemala, 57
Gulf of Mexico, 17, 47

Haiti, 39, 66, 67–68
Hawaii, 15
hemispheres, 41, 67, 83–84
Hidalgo, Miguel, 48
Hispaniola, 66, 67
Hitler, Adolf, 120
Honduras, 58
Hungary, 143, 185
hydroelectric power, 139, 171

Iceland, 139
Inca, 81

Indian Ocean, 5
Inuit, 27
Ireland, 103, 105–106
Italy, 100, 113, 129, 130–133, 139

Jamaica, 66, 103
Japan, 81, 83, 115
Jews, 99, 116, 124, 153, 179
John Paul II, Pope, 133, 152

Kiev, Ukraine, 171
Kohl, Helmut, 122

land reform, 89
Latin America, 39–94
    land and people of, 40–44
    problems of, 88–92
Latvia, 144, 169
Lithuania, 144, 169
London, England, 95, 99, 105, 108
L'Ouverture, Toussaint, 68
Lucid, Shannon, 20

Macedonia, 178
Maya, 57
Mediterranean climate, 112, 129, 148, 159, 177
Mediterranean Sea, 97, 112, 113, 129, 130, 139
Mendes, Chico, 76
mestizos, 42–43, 48, 57, 80, 81–82
Mexico, 34, 39, 40, 44, 47–51, 52, 56, 89, 92

Mexico City, Mexico, 39, 48, 49–50, 52
Moldovia, 170
Montenegro, 178
Montreal, Canada, 26, 29
Moscow, Russia, 143, 159, 161
mulattos, 73
Muslims, 99, 116, 161, 170, 171, 178–180

Native Americans, 10, 18, 27, 42–43, 48, 49, 57, 80, 81–82, 84
NATO, 137–138, 155, 180
Nicaragua, 57–58
Nicaragua, Lake, 58
North American Free Trade Agreement (NAFTA), 34–35
Northern Ireland, 103, 104, 106, 107
North European Plain, 98, 113, 123, 147, 152, 171
North Sea, 97, 104, 113, 123, 139
Norway, 138–139
nuclear energy, 114, 139
nuclear weapons, 170

oil, 17, 44, 49, 82, 84, 100, 105, 139, 148, 152, 160, 173
one-crop economy, 91

Pacific Ocean, 4–5, 9, 15, 27, 47, 56, 59–60, 84, 159

Panama, 57, 59–60
Panama Canal, 39, 59–60
Pan American Highway, 91
Paris, France, 99, 108, 113, 114, 115
Peru, 81–83, 84, 92
Poland, 120, 146, 148, 151–155, 185, 186
pollution, 35, 52, 75, 125, 139, 148, 172, 186, 187
Po River, 131
Portugal, 42, 73, 129, 130
Po Valley, 131
Protestant Church, 99, 107
Puerto Rico, 16, 66
Pyrenees Mountains, 113

Quebec, Canada, 28, 29

rain forest, 42, 47, 72, 74–75, 76
Rhine River, 99, 113, 123–124, 148
Rio Grande, 47, 48
Rocky Mountains, 9, 17, 24, 26
Roman Catholic Church, 43, 49, 73, 99, 106, 116, 130, 133, 152, 153, 178
Rome, Italy, 131, 132–133
Russia, 143–148, 153, 159–165, 169–173, 179, 184–187

St. Lawrence Lowlands, 26, 29
St. Lawrence River, 26, 29, 36

St. Lawrence Seaway, 35–36
St. Petersburg, Russia, 161
Sarajevo, Bosnia, 177, 179, 180
Sardinia, 130
Scotland, 103, 104, 105–106
Seine River, 113, 115
Serbia, 178, 179, 180
Serbs, 178–180
Siberia, 159, 160, 161, 162, 164, 165
Sicily, 130
Slovakia, 151
Slovenia, 178
Solar energy, 139
Solidarity, 153–154, 155
Soviet Union, 58, 121, 137, 145–147, 162–163, 169, 171–172, 186, 187
Spain, 10, 113, 129, 130
and Latin America, 42, 43, 48, 49, 52, 57, 66, 81
subsistence farming, 43, 49, 82, 88
Sweden, 139
Switzerland, 99–100, 113, 130, 139

Tenochtitlan, 52
terrorism, 83, 92
Thames River, 104, 105, 139
Tiber River, 132
Tito, Josip Broz, 178
Trans-Siberian Railroad, 143, 159, 160, 165

tundra, 160
Turkey, 138

Ukraine, 151, 170, 171–173
United Kingdom, 103–107, 139
United States, 7–12, 15–20, 33, 48, 49, 50–51, 58, 60, 66–67, 84, 115, 121, 138, 147, 154, 180
Ural Mountains, 147, 159, 160

Vatican City, 95, 132–133
Venezuela, 44
Vistula River, 152
volcanoes, 39, 41, 56–57, 58, 65, 130
Volga River, 160

Wales, 103, 104, 105–106
Walesa, Lech, 154, 155
Western Europe, 95–140, 147, 148, 151, 153, 154, 155, 180, 185
West Germany, 121–123
Witt, Katarina, 125
World War II, 114, 120–121, 124, 137, 145–146, 153, 178

Yeltsin, Boris, 163
Yugoslavia, 177–180